Leonard Bernstein's

Young People's Concerts

Edited by Jack Gottlieb

With an Introduction by Michael Tilson Thomas

AMADEUS PRESS

Leonard Bernstein's Young People's Concerts was originally published in 1962. This
revised and expanded edition is published by arrangement with The Leonard
Bernstein Office, Inc.

Published in 2005 by

AMADEUS PRESS, LLC
512 Newark Pompton Turnpike
Pompton Plains, New Jersey 07444, USA

For sales, please contact

NORTH AMERICA
AMADEUS PRESS, LLC
c/o Hal Leonard Corp.
7777 West Bluemound Road
Milwaukee, Wisconsin 53213, USA
Phone: 800-637-2852
Fax: 414-774-3259

UNITED KINGDOM AND EUROPE
ROUNDHOUSE PUBLISHING LTD.
Millstone, Limers Lane
Northam, North Devon EX39 2RG, UK
Phone: 01237-474474
Fax: 01237-474774
E-mail: roundhouse.group@ukgateway.net

E-mail: orders@amadeuspress.com
Website: www.amadeuspress.com

Book design by Claire Naylon Vaccaro
Illustrated by Madeline Sorel

All interior photographs of Leonard Bernstein courtesy of CBS, Inc. Reprinted by
permission of Video Education, Inc.

Cover photograph courtesy of The Leonard Bernstein Office, Inc.

Printed in the United States of America

Library of Congress Cataloging-in-Publication Data

Bernstein, Leonard, 1918-1990
  [Young people's concerts]
  Leonard Bernstein's young people's concerts / edited by Jack Gottlieb.-- 1st Amadeus
Press ed.
    p. cm.
  Includes bibliographical references (p.   ) and index.
  ISBN 1-57467-102-2
  1. Music appreciation--Juvenile literature. [1. Music appreciation.] I. Title: Young
people's concerts. II. Gottlieb, Jack. III. Title.

ML3928.B49 2005
781.1'7--dc22

                            2005024905

To my dearest own Young People
Jamie
Alexander
Nina

$\mathscr{C}$ONTENTS

Introduction to the New Edition

From the first moment I met Leonard Bernstein I understood that he was an asker of questions. "What is your favorite music?" "Why do you phrase it *that* way?" "How do you know that?" "Who's writing new good music and where can I hear it?" Questions were essential for him because questions led to answers, more knowledge, and, of course, to more questions. Over the years during our conversations I gathered that most of his thoughts on music could be condensed into three questions: What is happening? Why is it happening? What's the best way to communicate what's happening?

All these questions underlie the texts of his *Young People's Concerts*. Most of the titles begin with a "what"—and embedded in them are constant "why's," "how's," and "wherefore's."

Bernstein asked these questions for a reason. He believed that music is a language, a language one can learn to understand by examining its many components—be it the life story of composers, the function of intervals, or the characteristics of a style. All of his programs are really lessons in listening. Informed, active listeners are what he wants us to be—and his guidance is inspiring. He wants us to understand that the rich tradition of music is easily available to us and that the spontaneous joy we take in street cries, folk songs, show tunes, and rock and roll is equally in the music that, for lack of a better word, is called "classical."

These programs have great lasting appeal, even though they are period pieces. Sadly, Bernstein's assumptions about the range of knowledge and experience of his young listeners cannot be taken as much for granted today as when he made these shows. Some of his expressions, like "dollars to doughnuts," are as deliciously archaic as his references to "You Really Got Me" by The Kinks or The Association's "Along Comes Mary." But he had a purpose in making these references. He wanted to make "exact music"—as he prefers to call classical music—closer and more approachable to his audience. That message still sticks. He tackles all the "scary sounding" terms like sonata and cadenza and makes them understandable and fun.

Moreover, in the midst of the fun, there are messages of great importance to all music lovers. In the program called "What Does Music Mean?" he says:

> . . . there's no limit to the different kinds of feelings music can make you have. Some of those feelings are so special they can't even be described in words. Sometimes we can name the things we feel, like joy or sadness or love or hate or peacefulness. But there are other feelings so deep and special that we have no words for them, and that's where music is especially marvelous. It names the feelings for us, only in notes instead of words.

It seems amazing to us now that Bernstein convinced a major television network to invest the time and money to present as sophisticated and "non-commercial" a message as this—let alone a series that was so unswervingly dedicated to sharing the idea of artistic excellence.

Perhaps most touching about these programs is the enormous affection and feeling of connection to Bernstein and his message felt by the audiences who attended them or watched them on television. They still feel that today. There is a genuine desire on the part of those young people of yesteryear to share the message of these programs with their children and grandchildren. *There can be no greater tribute to an educator.*

—MICHAEL TILSON THOMAS, 2005

*E*ditor's Note

Twenty years have elapsed since Leonard Bernstein last presented a televised "Young People's Concert" with the New York Philharmonic. From 1958 to 1972, Bernstein wrote and appeared as commentator, piano-soloist, and conductor in fifty-three different concerts designed for young people (loosely defined as ages eight to eighteen). Bernstein's teaching skills and vivid personality soon became nationally known. Through print, audio, and visual media, he helped convert an entire generation of casual American music listeners into avid music lovers. His articulate and lucid talk was a most uncommmon attribute for a musician, who—as the saying goes—usually prefers to "let music speak [or should one say 'sing'?] for itself."

As a high school student he received a solid grounding in Latin (where else, but at the Boston Latin School?), and he was known to correct other people's grammar in the midst of heated discussions, usually to their chagrin. His natural affinity for foreign languages helped him communicate, in varying degrees of fluency, in German, French, Italian, Spanish, Yiddish, and Hebrew. His study was filled, floor to ceiling, with dictionaries, etymological works, and phrase books of all kinds. His familiarity with literature was almost frightening in its scope; and his passion for unconventional word games, like cutthroat anagrams and convoluted British-magazine crossword puzzles—the harder the better—almost bordered on the religious. At one time he had in his home an electronic box that randomly flashed on four letters at a blink, in unending different combinations. The purpose of this box was not to recognize the actual words that might have accidentally appeared, but instantaneously to infuse meaning into all the *non*-words through anagramming and supplying missing letters. Another game he played with companions, often during long car rides, was called "Mental Jotto," in which the challenge is to discover five-letter words through mental anagramming. He always won. This clearly was a musician whose interests and gifts ranged far beyond purely musical matters. A born teacher and eloquent spokesman on many wide-ranging issues, cultural and otherwise, he was intoxicated with words.

The popularity of the "Young People's Concerts" made bestsellers of the first two editions of the book based on them. These books have been too long out of print, and the demand for their reissue, as well as for that of the original concert videos, has been particularly heavy in the last decade. Nothing like them had been seen before 1958, and nothing since 1972 has come close to the record of their stunning achievement. There were other televised New York Philharmonic "Young People's Concerts" during and after the same fourteen-year Bernstein period, made by other personalities;[1] but none of them captured the public fancy with the same colorful impact. (To be fair, these other conductors did not have the time to develop a following, nor were they the Music Director of the Philharmonic.) Now, at long last, the public need for the Bernstein "Young People's Concerts" has been met. It was not possible for the last fifteen years because the web of clearances and rights created by performing organizations, artists, and publishers was enormously tangled. That web has finally been unraveled.

The Bernstein analyses and commentaries were, of course, more than ad-libbed introductory program notes to works being performed by the orchestra. Each concert was a carefully scripted event, eventually transcribed onto a TelePrompTer. Mr. Bernstein's practice was to write a first draft in pencil on yellow legal pads. These were then typed and distributed in a format with wide margins (computers were not then prevalent) designed for committee conferences. With Producer-Director Roger Englander, a team of production assistants[2] met with Mr. Bernstein in his home to review, discuss, clarify, time, and help rewrite portions of the script where needed. Possible cuts were suggested by the author himself, and often these had to be taken due to the time constraints of the approximately fifty-five minutes made available for airtime. (A total of about five minutes had to allotted to opening and closing credits and the commercial break for the hourlong concerts.) In the scripts newly added to this edition, some of these cut portions have been restored.

The family-type script meetings were miniworkshops, and were as exciting and fun-filled as the concerts themselves. There was a lot of easygoing give-and-take, with Bernstein welcoming the banter and commentary of his production team. But it must be emphatically stated that every word ultimately was his own. Given his impatience with misuse of language, it was a very rare instance, indeed, when he made an error. Therefore, when that did occur, it was a memorable happening. I recall, from 1964, one such rarity. During our meetings on the script for "Berlioz Takes a Trip" (included in this book), Maestro B. referred to a female wolf, a fantasy creature in the mind of Berlioz's hero in *Symphonie Fantastique*, as a "wolverine." But I protested: "How could a team of Michigan football players be known as a team of female anything?" He dismissed this objection cavalierly. The next day, however, he gave me a handwritten note. Apparently troubled by my comment, he had looked up the word, and wolverine turned out to be a badgerlike animal, not at all in the wolf family. It was replaced in the script with "wolf-girl." His note to me read:

> *To Jack Gottlieb, Esq.: I hereby testify that you were right, I was wrong. God bless you, you clever wolverine. Respectfully submitted, Leonard Bernstein, Ignoramus.*

I still have it among my prized papers.

Bernstein in his original *Foreword* makes mention of the problems that arise in transferring scripts that are spoken aloud to a medium that is read in silence. Not the least of these is what to do about musical excerpts that are intended to be heard live? Where possible, the newly added examples in this edition have been made as simple as those in the first edition. Again, to emphasize the author's original recommendation, in the case of full musical works or complete movements from larger works, the reader should make every effort to seek out recordings from libraries, private collections, on the radio, et al. We also urge the reader to look, in particular, for Bernstein/New York Philharmonic recorded interpretations, since these will generate some of the flavor of the actual telecasts.

All the concerts in this book have been, or soon will be, made available for home video libraries. In his Fore-word, Bernstein says that "examples and records have the advantage of letting you play them over and over again . . . as you cannot do, of course, on television"—in a statement, of course, that is no longer valid. Now, using video formats, it is equally possible to stop, reverse, and go forward—to play the music "over and over again for enjoyment and study." Nevertheless, the written page has the advantage of allowing readers of music to have hands-on "enjoyment"; and perhaps nonreaders of music will be motivated to"study." It becomes a matter of par-ticipatory involvement on the reader's part, something like the physical performances of the orchestral musicians who played the original concerts. In other words, this book challenges you not to be a couch potato.

The 1960s were a time of great social upheaval, with a moral character quite unlike that of previous decades. Television itself was among the major factors contrib-uting to the unrest: you only have to recall the funeral of John F. Kennedy and the Democratic National Con-vention in Chicago. The mystique of the 1960s, the decade of the Beatles, was closely allied with the so-called drug culture: LSD, Timothy Leary, flower chil-dren, hippies, and all the rest. In "Berlioz Takes a Trip," Maestro B. refers to psychedelic "trips" and hallucino-genics. But compared with the current generation's ac-quaintance with angel-dust, crack, and the like, the earlier decade's dalliance with drugs almost verges on romantic innocence. Nevertheless, for this new edition, it was decided to leave in all dated references. Not every young reader may be familiar with the music of the Kinks, or with the Beatles, although music like theirs is being nostalgically revived on certain radio stations in the 1990s.

With the passage of time, it is now possible to get an overview of Leonard Bernstein's musical mission. Those common themes that carried over from show to show, year to year, have been noted. Although he did feature program music (i.e., music with a story) in various concerts, one senses that he did so with reluctance—his main mission being to inculcate purely musical values, as opposed to extramusical ideas, into budding minds. It is for this reason that a script such as "Igor Stravinsky Birthday Party" is not included in this new edition, since the main body of that program was a retelling of the *Petrouchka* ballet story. But the story Berlioz reveals in *Symphonie Fantastique is* included because the concept of the *idée fixe* is a neat way of explaining the variation principle in musical composition. In his first book, *The Joy of Music,* Bernstein talks about the "Music Appreciation Racket" and of his desire to find a "happy medium" between that racket and "purely technical discussion." If ever anyone did find that happy medium, it must have been he.

—J.G., 1992

*F*oreword for

My Young Readers

Ever since we began to televise the New York Philharmonic Young People's Concerts back in 1958, requests have come in constantly for some way in which these programs might be preserved. This illustrated book is simply one way of meeting these many requests.

The change from television screen to printed page is not an easy one to accomplish. For one thing, we no longer have a big symphony orchestra handy, just waiting to jump in with examples at the drop of a baton. Instead, there are written-out musical examples, mostly made just as easy as possible to play on the piano. Every piece of music to which we refer in the course of the book has been recorded for the phonograph. I strongly recommend that whenever possible (especially for the more extensive examples under discussion) the reader provide himself with the appropriate recording. Both examples and records have the advantage of letting you play them over and over again for enjoyment and study, as you cannot do, of course, on television.

For another thing (and this is more subtle), the thoughts I have tried to get across to you when I spoke on television would have read slightly differently if taken down word for word in cold print—just differently enough so that a good deal of rewriting and editing has been necessary.

Then, too, there are a great many things to look at in a television show. One can *see* what instruments look like, for example, as well as *hear* them. In this book, therefore, we have pictures, and very imaginative they are.

The whole job of changing over from the television screen to printed book thus becomes something like translating from one language to another, or like orchestrating a piece of music written originally for piano alone. So if I don't always sound exactly like myself in print, you'll understand, won't you?

For this whole job of translation, I must thank first of all my colleague, Jack Gottlieb, who undertook the difficult job of making a first draft, and secondly a whole team of editors, designers, and artists working at Simon and Schuster under the general direction of my old friend Henry Simon, who had the idea of this book in the first place. I would also like to thank Mary Rodgers and Roger Englander for their great help to me in preparing and editing the original television programs, as well as their cohorts, Elizabeth Finkler and John Corigliano, Jr.

And above all, I would like to thank you young people for responding so warmly and intelligently to our programs; otherwise this book would never have been made.

—LEONARD BERNSTEIN, 1962

*L*eonard
*B*ernstein's

Young People's Concerts

*W*hat Does Music Mean?

What is any particular piece of music all about? For instance, what do you think this tune is about?

You will understand, I am sure, what my little daughter Jamie said when I played it for her. She said, "That's the Lone Ranger song, Hi-ho Silver! Cowboys and bandits and horses and the Wild West . . ."

Well, I hate to disappoint her, and you, too, but it isn't about the Lone Ranger at all. It's about notes: C's and A's and F's and even F-sharps and E-flats. No matter what stories people tell you about what music means, forget them. Stories are not what the music means. Music is never *about* things. Music just *is*. It's a lot of beautiful

1

notes and sounds put together so well that we get pleasure out of hearing them. So when we ask, "What does it *mean; what does this piece of music mean?*" we're asking a hard question. Let's do our best to answer it.

It's a funny thing about "meaning" in music. When you say, "What does it mean?" you're really saying, "What is it trying to tell me?" or "What ideas does it make me have?" It's just like words. When you hear words, you get ideas from them. If I shout, "Ouch, I burned my finger!" then you get certain ideas right away—

I burned my finger.

It hurts.

I may not be able to play the piano for some time.

I have a loud, ugly voice when I complain.

—lots of different ideas like that. Word-ideas.

But if I play you some notes on the piano, like this:

the notes won't give you any word-ideas. Notes aren't about burned fingers, or space travel, or lampshades, or anything.

What *are* they about? They're about music. For instance, take this little Prelude by Chopin:

It's beautiful music. But what is about? Nothing. Or take a passage from a Beethoven sonata:

That's not *about* anything, either. Or, again, a bit of jazz:

What's it about? Nothing. They're all about nothing, but they're all fun to listen to. Why should they be fun to listen to? I don't know. It's just a part of human nature to like to listen to music.

Notes, you see, aren't like words at all. Because if I say even one word all by itself, like "rocket," it means something. You get an idea right away. You see a picture in your mind.

Rocket. Bang!

But a note—one little note all alone:

means nothing. It's just plain old F-sharp—or B-flat:

It's a sound, that's all.

It's higher:

or lower:

LOUDER:

or softer:

It will be a different sound
if I play it on the piano, or
if I sing it, or if an oboe
plays it—

or a xylophone—

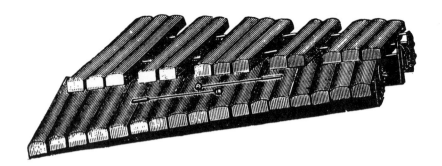

or a trombone.

These are all the *same* note, but with *different* sounds.

Now, all music is a combination of such sounds put together according to a plan. The person who plans it is the composer, whether he is called Rimsky-Korsakoff or Richard Rodgers. And his plan is to put the sounds together with rhythms and different instruments or voices in such a way that what finally comes out is exciting, or fun, or touching, or interesting, or all of these together.

That is what is called *music*, and what it means is what the composer planned. But it's a *musical* plan, so it has a *musical* meaning, and has nothing to do with any stories or pictures or anything of that sort.

Of course if there *is* a story connected with a piece of music, that's all right too. In a way, it gives an extra meaning to the music; but it's extra—like mustard with your hot dog. Mustard isn't part of the hot dog. It's extra. Well, the story isn't part of the music, either. And so, whatever the music really means, it's *not* the story—even if there is a story connected with it.

Now let's see if we can't find out what music *does* mean. Let's take the first step. You remember that piece we talked about at the beginning?

Do you still think that piece means the Wild West because it is the Lone Ranger tune? Well, it can't mean the Wild West for the simple reason that it was written by a man who never heard of the Wild West. He was an Italian named Rossini. We may *think* his music means horses and cowboys because we've been told so by the movies and television shows. But actually, Rossini wrote the music as an overture to the opera *William Tell*, which is about people in Switzerland—and that's pretty far from the Wild West. Everybody knows the story of William Tell, the man who had to shoot an apple off his little son's head with a bow and arrow.

You might, then, think that the music is supposed to be about William Tell and Switzerland instead of about cowboys. But it isn't that either. It's not about William Tell, or cowboys, or lampshades, or rockets, or anything like that which can be put down in words.

Then what makes it so exciting? A million reasons make it exciting, but they are all *musical* reasons. That's the main point.

For instance, take the rhythm:

Ta da *d*um, ta da *d*um Ta da *d*um *d*um *d*um

Beat it out with your knuckles on a wooden table, and it may remind you of the rhythm of galloping horses. Or beat it out on a snare drum, if you have one around the house, and it will sound like the rhythm of drums in a battle. But that doesn't mean the music is *about* horses or a battle. The meaning is only the excitement of that rhythm.

Another reason it's exciting is that it has a good tune, easy to remember. It starts with a phrase going up—as you can see by just looking at the notes even if you can't play them:

and then it answers itself with a phrase going down:

It's like a question and answer. Or maybe it's more like an argument, with the second person winning it. You might try this with a friend, singing back and forth at each other, and see who wins. First your friends sings the opening phrase, like this:

and you argue back with the second phrase:

Then he'll insist again with the third phrase (which is just like the first):

and then you clinch the argument with the last one, like this:

You win! You see what excitement there is in that last phrase? It has all the triumph and good feeling of winning an argument.

11

There are still more reasons why this music is exciting—the way it's played, or the instruments that play it. For instance, there are the violins who use their bows in a jumping way[1] to make the galloping sound. When all the strings do it together, the music really gallops! So you see, this music is exciting because it's written to be exciting, for *musical* reasons and no other reasons.

But you may wonder, then, why a composer gives names to his music at all. Why doesn't he just write something called "Symphony" or "Trio" or "Composition Number 28" or anything? Why does he give it a name like "The Sorcerer's Apprentice," or whatever it is, if it's not important to the music?

That is simply because every once in a while an artist will be stimulated to express himself by something outside himself—something he reads, or something that happens to him, or something he sees. Haven't you ever felt that way, that something happened to you that made you want to sing, or dance, or express your feelings in some way? Everyone knows that feeling. Well, it's the same with a composer.

Johann Strauss, for instance, wrote lots of waltzes. He called one of them "The Blue Danube," which you may know,[2] and which goes like this:

Now, the Danube River may have inspired Strauss to write the waltz, but those notes don't have anything to do with the river.

Another fine waltz by Strauss is called "Tales from the Vienna Woods," and has nothing to do with the woods of Vienna or any other woods. It could just as well have been called "The Blue Danube" or "The Emperor Waltz" or something else. A Strauss waltz by any other name is still just a lovely waltz. The name doesn't matter except to help you to tell one from the other and maybe give the music a little more color, like a fancy-dress costume.

Now I'm going to try a trick with you. I'm going to describe a piece of music that has a story, but I'm going to tell you the *wrong* story. It's just a story I made up to fit the piece of music, and I'll describe it without giving you its real name. And afterwards, when I tell you what it really is, you can perhaps get a recording and see how well the story fits.

Here goes: In the middle of a big city stands an enormous jail, full of prisoners. It's midnight and they're all asleep except for one who can't sleep because he's innocent; he was put in jail unjustly. He spends the whole night practicing on his kazoo while the other prisoners snore all around him. But this kazoo-playing prisoner has a friend who is going to come tonight and rescue him— Superman! So Superman comes charging along through the alley on his motorcycle; and you hear the strings make the charge:

Then he whistles his secret whistle (in the woodwinds) so the prisoner will know he's coming, like this:

As he gets near the prison, he hears all the prisoners snoring away peacefully in the dead silence of night, which the brass imitate by fluttering their tongues as they blow:

And he also hears his friend playing his kazoo over the snoring, which gets louder as he gets nearer:

Suddenly he charges into the prison yard and bops the guard over the head, done in the orchestra with a loud bang in the percussion—like this:

The kazoo stops playing, and with all the snoring still going on, Superman grabs his friend and carries him away on his motorcycle. The snoring gets farther and farther away, until we don't hear it any more—and, with a burst from the orchestra, our hero at last reaches freedom!

15

All that makes good sense, doesn't it? But it's not the real story at all. The music is actually part of a much longer piece, *Don Quixote* by Richard Strauss (no relation to Johann Strauss), and Strauss is trying to tell an entirely different story in this music, which is something like this:

Don Quixote is a foolish old man who lived back in the days when knights on horseback were rapidly going out of fashion. He has read too many books about knighthood and conquering armies for beautiful ladies, and finally he decides he is a marvelous knight himself. So off he goes on his skinny old horse to conquer the world:

He has with him a companion named Sancho Panza, a fat, jolly little fellow who is very faithful to his master, but who is sensible enough to know that his master is a little cuckoo. And so we hear Sancho chuckling to himself:

They are riding together when they see a flock of sheep in the field going *baa-baa*:

And with them is a shepherd playing on his pipe, as all shepherds do:

Don Quixote, in his mixed-up mind, thinks the sheep are an army specially put there for him to conquer, so in he charges and cuts them down:

17

And the sheep run off in all directions, baaing wildly. He is convinced he has done a truly knightly deed, and is he proud!

By now you've certainly realized that the same music which sounded right for Superman on his motorcycle was really Don Quixote on his horse; that the prisoner playing his kazoo was actually the shepherd playing on a pipe. What's the difference whether this:

is the sound of snoring prisoners or of baaing sheep? Or whether this:

is Superman bopping the guard, or Don Quixote bopping the sheep? And so on and so forth.

There are, in fact, a hundred other stories I could have made up about this piece, but the music would still have been just as good or just as bad as it is *without any story at all.* Now do you see what I mean? The same music might express very different things.

Later in this same *Don Quixote* there is a part about another adventure the old fellow has, when he and his friend Sancho Panza have a wild ride through the air. In this part there is even a wind machine in the orchestra to give you the feeling of the wind whistling by as they whoosh up and down through the clouds. But why couldn't this music be describing the flight of a jet plane? Or a satellite moon whistling around in its orbit, or even some old giant snoring? It doesn't matter what it's about; it's exciting music because the music is exciting.

Now, that's enough talk about music that tells stories. Let's next take a giant step toward finding out what music *does* mean by listening to some music that doesn't try to tell a story but only to paint some sort of picture or describe an atmosphere: the look or feel of something— like a sunrise, or a night in the woods, or an old haunted house. This is getting closer to real musical meaning, because there's no story to worry about while we're listening. All we have to think of is the general idea of the picture. We can concentrate more on the music and enjoy it more.

Take Beethoven's *Sixth Symphony,* for instance. Here is a wonderful piece, full of fine tunes and great rhythms and marvelous spirit—happy, driving, peaceful—all kinds of things. But in Beethoven's mind this symphony was tied up with the idea of the countryside—farmers

and brooks and birds and shepherds. So he called it the "Pastoral" symphony. As you know, "pastoral" means anything to do with the country.

At the beginning of the first movement he wrote the words, "Awakening of cheerful feelings on arriving in the country." It is played quietly on the strings and goes like this:

It certainly does sound happy, cheerful, pretty. But these feelings could be happy for any other reason too. Supposing Beethoven had written in the score, "Happy feelings because my uncle left me a million dollars,"—he could still have composed this happy music, and it would be just as good, just as happy.

Beethoven calls the second movement of this symphony "By the Brook." The motion of the music is supposed to imitate or suggest the motion of water in a brook. It goes like this:

But suppose we called it "Asleep in the Hammock," and thought of the motion as one of quiet rocking instead of

21

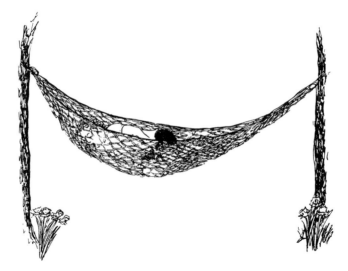

water. It wouldn't make any difference, and the music would be just as pleasant and satisfying.

One of the best pieces that paint pictures is by the Russian composer Moussorgsky, who wrote *Pictures at an Exhibition*. What Moussorgsky did was to take a lot of pictures hanging on the wall in a museum and write a set of piano pieces he thought would describe them—in other words, he tried to do with notes what his friend, the painter Victor Hartmann, had done with paint. Then the famous French composer Ravel changed these piano pieces into orchestra pieces, thus giving them even more descriptive color. Of course, notes can't do what paint can do. You can't draw a nose with notes, or a building, or a sunset. But you can *sort* of do it.

For example, one of those Moussorgsky pictures shows children playing in a park, and what Moussorgsky did to make it sound like children playing was to imitate in notes the way kids talk when they play games—which is almost like singing—

Al- lee al- lee in come free !

or when they are making fun of each other, and go, "Nya, nya, nya, nya." But here is how Ravel does it, by using nasal-sounding woodwinds:

Then there's another picture Moussorgsky painted with notes—of many little chicks not yet out of their shells. With a lot of short, cheepy notes in the woodwinds, Moussorgsky and Ravel imitated the squawking and pecking—like this:

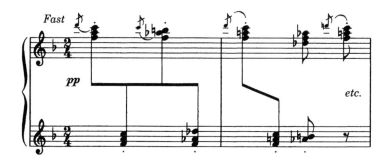

In another picture he painted a big gate in the city of Kiev, a tremendous stone structure.

You can see what Moussorgsky had in his mind when you hear the big, heavy chords—with the full orchestra—like pillars holding up those tons of stone:

23

Design for the ballet Trilbi: "Chick in Shell" (from
Hartmann's original in the Institute of Literature, Len-
ingrad). THE BETTMANN ARCHIVE.

Engraving of the Great Gate of Kiev, topped by the emblem of Russia. THE BETTMANN ARCHIVE.

It makes you think of a big gate, but only because you were told so. If you had been told, instead, to think of the Mississippi River flowing majestically down the middle of America, you would have seen that in your mind. So here we have the old question again: The picture that goes with music goes with it *only because the composer says so,* but it's not really part of the music. It's extra.

Keep that in mind when you listen to recordings of the "Ballet of the Unhatched Chicks" and "The Great Gate of Kiev" from *Pictures at an Exhibition* by Moussorgsky.

Now we're going to take another giant step toward finding out the answer to our original question, "What does music mean?" And this is a really big step. We're getting closer now to the answer.

Let's forget about all the music that tells stories or paints pictures, and think about music that describes emotions, feelings—like pain, happiness, anger, loneliness, excitement or love. I guess most music is like that; and the better it is, the more it will make you feel the emotions that the composer felt when he wrote it.

Tchaikovsky was a composer who did this—who always tried to have his music mean something emotional. Take the theme from his *Fourth Symphony* that goes like this:

Perhaps the best way to describe it is to say that it has the feeling of wanting very badly something that you can't have. Did you ever feel you wanted something more than anything else in the world, and you said so, but they said No, and you said it again: "I *want* it!" And again they said No, and again you said, louder and more excited, "I *want* it!" and again more excited, "I *want* it!" until it seemed that something would break inside you and there was nothing left to do but cry? This is what happens in this passage:

26

I want it,_____ I want __ it,_____ I want it,_____ *etc.*

If you listen to it played by an orchestra, I'm sure you will have those same emotions.

Sometimes Tchaikovsky uses the same tune to describe two different emotions. For instance, at the beginning of his *Fifth Symphony* he writes this tune, which sounds sad and gloomy and depressed, especially as it is played by the clarinets:

But at the end of the symphony, he changes a couple of notes—what musicians call changing from minor to major (see Chapter Fourteen on modes)—and the whole orchestra comes out sounding joyful and triumphant, like someone who has just made a touchdown and is the hero of the football game:

Listening to that music makes you feel triumphant!

And now we can really understand what the meaning of music is. *It's the way it makes you feel when you hear it.* Finally, we've taken the last giant step, and we're there; we know what music means now. We don't have to know everything about sharps and flats and chords to understand music. If it tells us something—not a story or a picture, but a feeling—if it makes us change inside, then we are understanding it. That's all there is to it. Because those feelings belong to the music. They're not *extra,* like the stories and pictures we talked about before; they're not outside the music. They're what music is about.

And the most wonderful thing of all is that there's no limit to the different kinds of feelings music can make you have. Some of those feelings are so special they can't even be described in words. Sometimes we can name the things we feel, like joy or sadness or love or hate or peacefulness. But there are other feelings so deep and special that we have no words for them, and that's where music is especially marvelous. It names the feelings for us, only in notes instead of words.

It's all in the way music moves. We must never forget that music is movement, always going somewhere, shifting and changing and flowing from one note to another. That movement can tell us more about the way we feel than a million words can.

For instance, if you play just one note for a long time—

—it means nothing by itself; it's not moving. But the minute another note is played after it—

—right away there's a meaning: a meaning we can't name, something like a stretching or a pushing or a pulling, whatever you want to call it. (See also Chapter Ten on melody and Chapter Thirteen on intervals.) The meaning is the way the music moves, and it makes something happen inside you. If I move from that first note to a different one—

—the meaning changes. Something else happens inside you. The stretch is bigger somehow, and stronger.

Now this note:

means one thing with this chord under it:

and it makes you feel a certain way, but it means something else with this other chord under it:

And it means something else still with this chord:

and makes you have a different feeling.

These notes mean something spooky and exciting is going to happen, as in old movies:

but the same notes played in a different way mean something sweet and waltzy:

So you see, the meaning of music is to be found *in* music, in its melodies, in its harmonies, in its rhythms, in its orchestra color, and especially in the way it *develops* itself.

But the way music develops itself is a whole other discussion, and I am going to have something to say about it when we talk about symphonic music. Right now all I mean to point out is that music has its own meanings, right there for you to feel inside the music; and you don't need any stories or pictures to tell what it means. If you like music at all, you'll find out the meanings for yourselves, just by listening. And that's what you should do. Sit back and relax, enjoy it, listen to the notes, feel them move around, jumping, hopping, bumping, flashing, sliding—and just enjoy THAT.

The meaning of music is in the music, and nowhere else.

*W*hat Makes Music American?

I don't think there's anyone in the country— or in the world, for that matter—who wouldn't know right away that Gershwin's music—say, *An American in Paris*—is American music. It's got "America" written all over it—not just in the title, and not just because the composer was American. It's in the music itself: it *sounds* American, smells American, makes you feel American when you hear it.

Now, why is that? What makes certain music seem to belong to America, belong to us?

Almost every country, or nation, has some kind of music that belongs to it, and sounds right and natural for its people. When a nation has it own kind of music, we call it "nationalistic" music. Sometimes it's just folk music, very simple songs—or not even *songs*: maybe just prayers for rain banged out on Congo drums:

or a sort of primitive chanting, in the Arab style:

or it can be dance music, like a mazurka from Poland:

or a tarantella from Italy:

or it could be a reel from Ireland:

The minute you hear that reel you know it's Irish music, just as you know the mazurka is Polish and the tarantella is Italian.

You couldn't mistake a Spanish rhythm in a million years. For instance, in the *Spanish Rhapsody* by Ravel, the rhythm, with the sound of the castanets or the tambourine, makes the music definitely Spanish in character:

A Brahms *Hungarian Dance* is as Hungarian as goulash:

Or take this example from Tchaikovsky's *Fourth Symphony*:

It's Russian because it has a Russian folk song in it, an old tune that all Russians know and have sung since they were kids. It's called "The Little Birch Tree," and it goes like this:[1]

Tchaikovsky used this tune extensively in his *Fourth Symphony*, and that settles *that* symphony. It's Russian.

So now you can see that when this kind of music is played in the country it belongs to, all the people listening to it feel that it belongs to them, and that they belong to it—it's *their* music. Because in most countries the people have been singing the same little tunes for hundreds of years, they own them. They have inherited them from their forefathers, who got them from *their* forefathers. So when the Russians hear a Tchaikovsky symphony, they feel closer to it than, say, a Frenchman does, or than we do.

But in America our forefathers came from many different countries. Take, for example, the ancestors of some of America's leading composers. Howard Hanson's parents came from Sweden. Walter Piston's from Italy and George Gershwin's from Russia, while Charles Ives came from a long line of New England whalers, originally British. And if we were to find out the ancestry of all the Americans reading this book, I am sure it would take us to every country in the world.

So, with all these different forefathers we have, what is it we all have in common that we could call *our* folk music? That's a tough question. We haven't had very much time to develop a folk music. Don't forget, America is a very new country, compared to all those others. We're not even two hundred years old yet![2]

Actually, our really serious American music didn't begin until about seventy-five years ago. At that time the few American composers we had just imitated the European composers, like Brahms, Liszt, and Wagner. We might call this the kindergarten period of American music. For instance, there was a very fine composer named George W. Chadwick, who wrote expert music, and even deeply felt music; but you almost can't tell it apart from Brahms or Wagner.

But around the beginning of the twentieth century, American composers were beginning to feel self-conscious about not writing American-*sounding* music. And it took a foreigner to make them feel it. He was the Czechoslovakian composer Dvořák, who came here on a visit, and was amazed to find all our composers writing the same kind of music *he* wrote. So he said to the American composers, "Look, why don't you use your own folk music when you write? You've got marvelous stuff here—the music of the Indians, who are the *real* native Americans. Use it!" But he was forgetting the important thing, that Indian music has nothing to do with most of us, whose forefathers were not Native Americans; and so Indian music is simply not our music.

But Dvořák didn't worry about that; and he got so excited that he decided to write an American symphony himself, and show us how it could be done. So he made up some Native American themes (and some African-American themes, because he decided also that black folk music was American), and he wrote a whole "*New World*" *Symphony* around those themes. But the trouble is that the music doesn't *sound* American at all. It sounds Czech, which is how it should sound, and very pretty it is, too. I'm sure you know the second movement of the symphony—a famous tune that is often called "Goin' Home."[3]

Most people think it's a Negro spiritual, and it's often sung that way. But it isn't black spiritual at all; it's a nice Czech melody by Dvořák. There's nothing Negro or American about it. In fact, if I put words about Czechoslovakia to it, it could sound like the Czech national anthem:

Czech - o - slo - va - ki - a,   How I long for Thee!

No - ble hills, rocks and rills,   land so dear to me.

Doesn't sound very American, does it?

In spite of this, Dvořák made a big impression on the American composers of his time. They all got excited too, and began to write hundreds of so-called American pieces with Native American and African-American melodies in them. It became a disease, almost an epidemic. Everyone was doing it. And most of those Montezuma operas and Minnehaha symphonies and Cotton-pickin' suites are dead and forgotten, and gathering dust in old libraries. You can't just *decide* to be American; you can't just sit down and say, "I'm going to write American music, if it kills me"; you can't be nationalistic on purpose. That was the mistake; but it was a natural mistake to make at the beginning. Those early composers were just learning to be Americans. They were just graduating from that kindergarten into grammar school.

Even out of this grammar-school period came some pretty fine American music—by Edward MacDowell, for instance. Among other things, he wrote a suite that uses Indian folk material in it, but I still can't say that it sounds really American to me. It's more like our old friend Dvořák.

Then there was a composer named Henry Gilbert, who was also very talented, but who was more interested in Negro themes. And there were many others. But there was still no real American music.

Now our American composers were about to graduate from grammar school and enter high school. By this time the First World War was over, and something new and very special had happened in American music. Jazz had been born and it changed everything.

At last there was something like an American folk music that belonged to *all* Americans. Jazz was everybody's music. Everybody danced the fox trot and knew how to sing "Alexander's Ragtime Band," whether he came from Texas, North Dakota or South Carolina. So any *serious* composer growing up in America at that time couldn't keep jazz out of his ears or out of his music. It was part of him; it was in the air he breathed. A composer like Aaron Copland began to write pieces like *Music for the Theatre*, which is filled with jazz ideas, and they were played not by jazz bands or dance orchestras but by great musical organizations like the Boston Symphony Orchestra. What a shock the Bostonians must have had hearing Copland's jazz in Symphony Hall over thirty years ago!

This rage for jazz was so strong that even European composers began using it in their music—composers like Ravel, even Stravinsky.

But certainly, the composer who used jazz most effectively was Gershwin. When he wrote his *Rhapsody in Blue* in 1924, he rocked the town of New York, and then the whole country, and finally the whole civilized world. Imagine how this must have sounded to the ears of those serious music-lovers way back then:

41

Here at last was a real and natural folk influence—
jazz—much realer and much more natural than Native
American music or African-American spirituals could
ever be. But our composers were still in high school, so

to speak; and by that I mean they were still being American *on purpose*. Only now they were using *jazz* to be American, instead of Native American and Creole themes. They were still trying consciously to write

"American" music—and the results were still not very natural. But during the thirties the jazz influence became a part of their living and breathing, and the composers didn't even have to think twice about it. They just wrote music, and it came out American all by itself. That was much better. That was leaving high school and going to college.

For instance, take the rhythms of jazz. The thing that makes jazz rhythms so special is something called *syncopation*, which means getting an accent where you don't expect it—or getting a strong beat where a weak beat should be. For example, here are some regular, even beats—four to a bar:

On top of those steady beats let's put some off-beat notes, or syncopations, in between and against them:

And this is how the Charleston rhythm goes, in which the syncopation comes after the second beat:

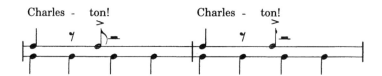

Now, back in what we called the high-school days, composers would use those syncopated beats in their music just like jazz, as in the Copland and Gershwin music. But after a while, in the thirties, those syncopations became *part* of the music—so much so that the music doesn't even sound like jazz any more. In other words, it was no longer using syncopation "on purpose," but just by accident, by habit. We now get a brand-new American rhythm, which comes out of jazz but doesn't sound like jazz at all. By now, it's become a natural part of our musical speech. For instance, a composer named Roger Sessions writes a piece for organ, a chorale prelude. A "chorale prelude" is a serious piece with a religious atmosphere. That's the last place in the world where you'd expect to find syncopated accents. But there they are, deep in the music, making it American, but without sounding like jazz:

That just couldn't be music by a European.

It's like the English language spoken with an American accent. It's the accent that makes it different—almost like a whole other language. The accent, the rhythm, the speed all come out of our way of moving and living. Just think what a difference there is between the English spoken by the British poet Keats and the English of an American poet! It's really the same language they're speaking. The words look the same on paper, but they *sound* utterly different. Listen to Keats:

Bright Star, would I were steadfast as thou art!
Not in lone splendor hung aloft the night,
And watching, with eternal lids apart,
Like Nature's patient, sleepless eremite,
The moving waters at their priestlike task
Of pure ablution round earth's human shores, . . .

Now compare that English with this English by the American poet Kenneth Fearing:

And wow he died as wow he lived,
   going whop to the office and blooie
   home to
   sleep and
   biff got married and bam had children
   and
   oof got fired,
zowie did he live and zowie did he die, . . .

Almost like two different languages, aren't they?

Well, something like that happened to American music. The jazz influence grew to be such a deep part of our musical language that it changed the whole sound of our music. Take a simple horn call, for example. Music has always been full of horn calls, or bugle calls, or trumpet calls. Now, here's the way Beethoven used a horn call in his *Third Symphony*, a fine old European way:

And here's the way the "Bugle Call Rag," a popular American song, uses the same notes—but they come out more like a Louis Armstrong horn call:

With swing

I don't want to give you the idea that jazz is the whole story. Actually it's only a small part of it, though an

extremely important one. There are many other things about American music that make it sound American— things that have nothing to do with jazz, but have to do with different sides of our American personality. One of the main personality traits in our music is the one of youth—loud, strong, and wildly optimistic. William Schuman is a composer who is a perfect example of this quality. His *American Festival Overture* is full of rip-roaring vitality, and reminds you of kids having a marvelous time. In fact, this overture was based on a street call that

47

Schuman used when he was a kid, when the fellows used to call each other to come out and play: "Wee-aw-kee!" Some of you may remember that call from the "Lassie" show. This is how Schuman used it in his overture:

That's vitality for you! Nothing depressed or gloomy about our American Schuman.

Then there's another kind of American vitality, not so much of the city, but belonging more to the rugged West, and full of pioneer energy. The music of Roy Harris has this kind of vitality.

SYMPHONY NO. 3

Somehow that ruggedness is American in its feeling.

Then there's a kind of loneliness to be found in a lot of American music that's different from other kinds of loneliness. You find it in the way the notes are spaced out very far apart, like the wide open spaces that our huge country is full of. Here, for example, is a short quotation from Copland's ballet *Billy the Kid*, a section which describes a quiet night on the prairie:

Can you hear that wide-open feeling? That's really American, too.

Then there's a sweet, simple, sentimental quality that gets into our music from hymn-singing—especially from Southern Baptist hymns. We can find lots of this kind of very American naïve quality in the music of Virgil Thomson, who comes from Kansas City. Here's a bit from one of his operas, called *The Mother of Us All*, which has that sweet, homespun, American quality:

Then we have another kind of sentimentality that comes out of our popular songs—a sort of crooning pleasure, like taking a long warm bath. Here's a part of Randall Thompson's *Second Symphony*, which is almost like a song Sinatra sings:

In fact, there are so many qualities in our music that it would take much too long to list them. There are as many sides to American music as there are to the American people—our great, varied, many-sided democracy. And perhaps that's the main quality of all: the many-sidedness. Think of all the races and personalities from all over the globe that make up our country. When we think of that we can understand why our own folk music is so complicated. We've taken it all in: French, German, Scotch, Italian, African, Scandinavian, and all the rest, learned it from one another, borrowed it and stolen it and cooked it all up in a melting pot. So what our composers are nourished on finally is a folk music that is probably the richest in the world, and all of it is American, whether it's jazz, or square-dance tunes, or cowboy songs, or hillbilly music, or rock 'n' roll, or Cuban mambos, or Mexican huapangos, or Missouri hymn-singing. It's like all the different accents we have in our speaking; there's a little Mexican in some Texas accents, and a little Swedish in the Minnesota accent, and a little Slavic in the Brooklyn accent, and a little Irish in the Boston accent. But it's all American, just like Copland's *Billy the Kid*, which also has a Mexican accent here and a Brooklyn accent there. If you listen to a recording of this, you'll hear the sweet, slow cowboy drawl in the first tune, then rip-roaring American rhythms in the gunfight that follows, and finally, the honky-tonk sound of an old-fashioned Western saloon. And hearing all these "accents," you can feel strongly what it means to be an American—a descendant of all the nations on the earth.

*W*hat Is

Orchestration?

The word *orchestration* means a lot of different things to different people. Let's try to clear some of them up. I think you'll find this one of the most exciting subjects in all music.

Mainly, orchestration is the department of music that deals with the ways in which a composer arranges his music to be played by an orchestra, whether it's an orchestra of 7, 17, 70—or 107 (which is the size of a big modern symphony orchestra).

Of course, this arranging isn't always done by the composer himself. For instance, in most Broadway shows, the composer is the man who writes the songs—Cole Porter or Irving Berlin, for example; but then someone you've probably never heard of comes along and arranges those songs for the orchestra to play.[1] He's called the *orchestrator,* but we're not concerned with him. We're going to talk only about orchestration that's done by the original composer. Composers of concert music almost always do their own orchestration, naturally, because orchestrating is really a *part* of composing, and a very important part.

Let's look at a piece by the Russian composer named Rimsky-Korsakoff, who is regarded as the real master of orchestration, the one who wrote the most famous book about it, and the one so many other composers have imitated ever since. Almost any piece at all by Rimsky-Korsakoff is a model for making the orchestra shine brilliantly through many different combinations of sound, one after another. At the same time, his orchestration never interferes with the clarity of the music itself, just for the sake of exciting sounds. That's not so easy as it may seem.

Let's examine, on the facing page, a page of his *Capriccio Espagnole*, or *Spanish Caprice*.

That whole page full of notes contains only *four* bars of music! But it tells us in detail what every instrument in the orchestra is doing for those four little bars.

How did Rimsky-Korsakoff arrive at this page? Well, to begin with, the music, as he heard it in his head, was made up of four different ideas. First of all, the big tune:

Heavy and Dance-like

—then the Spanish rhythm in the accompaniment:

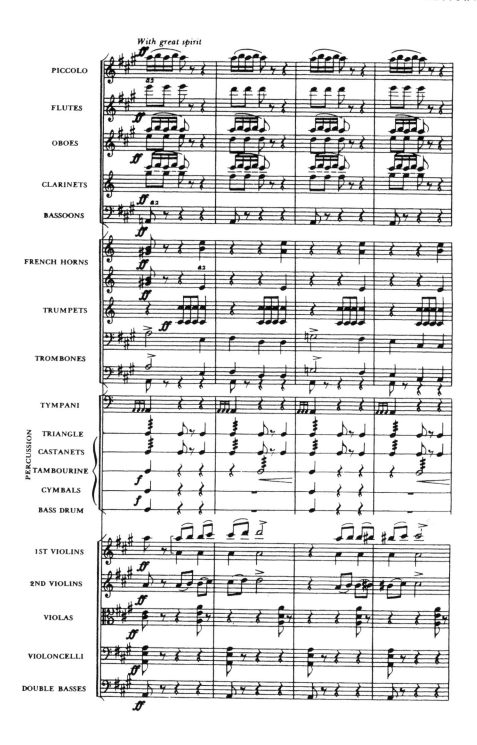

—then another little tune that goes along with it:

—and finally, this other Spanish rhythm in the accompaniment:

Now, he was faced with the job of writing all that down for a symphony orchestra of a hundred-odd men to play so that all four ideas mesh together, clear and strong and exciting. And so he distributed the four ideas to the orchestra this way:

He gave the big tune to the trombones:

and the other little tune that goes along with it to the violins:

And the first Spanish rhythm he divided between the woodwinds and the horns:

The other Spanish rhythm he divided between the tympani (along with other bass instruments) and the trumpets:

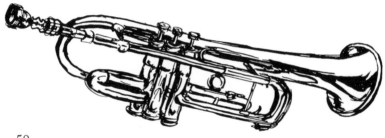

And then he added all these percussion instruments to emphasize the Spanish-dance flavor of the rhythm:

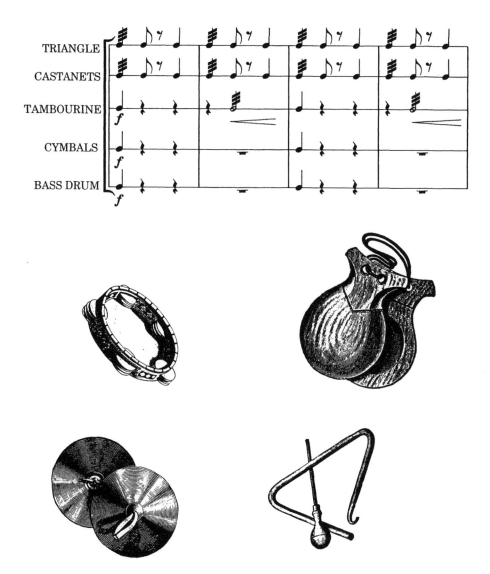

So, all together, the four bars look like this to the conductor:

And that sounds just fine when it's played. What Rimsky-Korsakoff did was to take the bare notes in his head and dress them up. But *good* orchestration is not only dressing up the music. It's got to be the *right* orchestration for that particular piece of music, like the right suit or right dress. Bad orchestration means something like putting on a sweater to go swimming.

So remember, what *good* orchestration means is orchestration that's exactly right for that music and lets it be heard in the clearest, most effective way.

Of course, that's pretty hard to do. Just think of what a composer has to know before he can orchestrate a piece he's written. First, he has to understand how to handle each instrument separately—to know what it can do and what it can't, what are its lowest and highest notes, its good and not-so-good notes, and all the different sounds it can make. Then he has to understand how to handle different instruments together, how to blend them, and how to balance them. He has to be careful that some instruments which are bigger and louder, like the trombone, don't drown out the littler, softer instruments, like the flute, Or that the percussion section doesn't drown out the strings. Or, if he's writing for a theater or opera orchestra, he has to see that his instruments don't drown out the singers.

Then he has to be careful about mixing the instruments so they don't get muddy-sounding—and lots of other problems like that. But the biggest problem he has is to *choose.* Imagine yourself sitting down to orchestrate a piece you've written, with 107 instruments of all kinds waiting for you to decide which one should play when!

You can see how hard it is for a composer to make up his mind and choose among all those instruments; to say nothing of the hundreds and millions of possible *com-*

binations of all those instruments. For instance, there is a famous flute solo at the beginning of Debussy's *Afternoon of a Faun*. What made Debussy decide on the flute—just the flute—to begin that piece? He knew what he wanted, what his *music* wanted, and that meant the flute, with its sweet, pale, airy sound. If he had picked the trumpet to do that tune, it would have sounded altogether different—too bright, too rich, and not at all so delicate and afternoonish. It would be the wrong piece of clothing.

Or take the beginning of Gershwin's *Rhapsody in Blue*, which, as you know, is that peculiar sliding wail by the clarinet. Imagine that wail played by a viola, for instance. It would sound pretty silly. The whole feeling of jazz goes out the window. Or imagine a Bach *Brandenburg Concerto* for strings played by brass instead of strings—which might not be so bad, but it's obviously not what Bach meant by his music.

So you see, it's an important part of a composer's job to choose his instruments, because it is those instruments which have to carry his music to your ears. And there are so many possibilities! Just to give you an idea, try an experiment in orchestrating yourselves.

Make up a tune of your own—it can be as simple or silly as you want. Then try to decide how it should be orchestrated—you yourself are the one to decide! Test it first with the sound *oo*, soft and moaning, like an organ, or low clarinets. Is that sound right? Maybe, maybe not. Perhaps it needs a strong sound: try that by just humming or buzzing softly. Or it might need a *loud* string sound: *zoom, zoom, za-zoom*. Or perhaps what's right is the *tick-tick-tick* of high woodwinds, playing short and sharp. Try *that*. Or the *ta-ka-ta-ka-ta* of trumpets. Or the *doodle-oodle* of flutes. Or the loud, heavy buzzing of muted horns.

Or . . . there are so many! And you may find that the
right answer lies in no one of these, but in a combination
of two, or more, of these sounds, like the *doodle-oodle* of
flutes *and* the humming of strings, together.

There's another experiment that's good to try, especially when you go to bed, before falling asleep. Try to
hear—in your *mind's ear*—some bit of music, any musical
sound; and then try to decide what *color* it makes you
think of. Musical sounds do seem to have colors—at

least, many people think so.[2] For instance, when you sing *oo* it seems to me sort of bluish in color. But when you *hum*, the color is darker and warmer, like a deep red—or so it seems to me. And when you sing *ta-ka-ta* it seems to me like a fiery orange. I can really *see* the colors in my mind. Can you? Lots of people see colors when they hear music; and these colors are part of the *orchestration*.

So, with all these millions of colors to choose from, the composer really has a job. How does he go about it? There are two ways to go about it: one is by writing only for instruments that belong to the same family. This would mean an orchestra of *only* strings or *only* woodwinds, and so on. The other way is to mix up the instruments, putting members of different families together, as, for instance, cellos and oboes. That would be more like the regular symphony orchestra.

The first way is more homey, like a gathering of family relations. The second is more like going out and getting together with friends.

What do we mean by "families"? You have probably heard that word "family" used over and over again whenever the orchestra was being described, especially at children's concerts. You're always hearing about the woodwind family, with Mama clarinet, Grandfather bassoon, Little Sister piccolo, and Big Sister flute, Uncle English horn, and Auntie oboe—and all the rest of them. Well, in spite of all that awful babytalk, it's still true that these woodwinds *are* a sort of family. They're related because they're all played by blowing wind into them, and they're all—well, almost all—made of wood. So they're called *woodwinds*. They all sit near one another on the concert stage, and behave like a family. And they have all kinds of cousins, too—different kinds of clari-

64

nets, for instance, like the little E-flat clarinet, and the bass clarinet. And then there are saxophones, and the alto flute, and the oboe d'amore, and the contra bassoon.

It's a long list. And there's even a group of *second cousins*, the French horns, which are made of brass, and so really ought to belong to the brass family. But they blend so well with *either* the woodwinds *or* the brass that they are related to both families—rather like in-laws.

Now that we've met this big wind family, let's see how they can be used in orchestration. The minute one of them begins to play—even if he's playing all by himself— then we're already dealing with orchestration. For instance, the part in Prokofieff's *Peter and the Wolf* where the cat is being described—you know that funny little melody on the clarinet?

Now, that by itself is a piece of expert orchestration because no other instrument in the whole woodwind section is so perfectly right for cat music. It's so velvety and dark and—well, catlike. So Prokofieff had to make a choice: he chose the clarinet, and that was good orchestrating. And, in the same piece, he chose the oboe to represent the duck. What could be a better quacking sound than an oboe playing this?

Things get more exciting as we begin to put different members of the family together in groups. For instance, there are woodwind quintets—for five instruments—which *sound* just like a family. They go with each other so naturally; and even though they all have different sounds, or colors, they're enough alike so that they blend.

A good example of this blending is Hindemith's *Kleine Kammermusik* (Little Chamber Music) for wind quintet. Then there are even bigger family reunions—such as Mozart's *Serenade for Thirteen Wind Instruments*. What a delicious blend they make! And the family can get so big that it begins to sound more like what we think of as an orchestra, not just a chamber group. But it's still a family orchestra—they're all woodwinds. The great modern composer Stravinsky has even written a symphony for a whole orchestra of winds.

Well, that's enough of the wind family for a while. Let's have a look at another family—an enormous one called the strings; and let's see how they can be used. We use only four kinds of stringed instruments: the violins, which of course you can easily recognize; then the violas, which look like violins but are a little bigger and sound a little lower; the cellos, which are even bigger and lower; and the double basses, the biggest and lowest. Again, it's the same story. Even if one lonely violin is playing, the composer has to *orchestrate* for him. This may sound silly to you—orchestrating for one lone instrument—but it *is* orchestrating in miniature. This is because even with one instrument the composer has the problem of choosing. First he has to choose the violin itself, instead of any number of other instruments, for that particular music he hears in his head. Then he has lots of other choices to make, like which of the four strings to play on; in what direction the bow should move, up or down; whether the bow should bounce (remember, musicians call it *spiccato*),[3] or go smoothly (*le-*

gato), or maybe not even be used at all (that is, the strings are plucked with the fingers, or *pizzicato*); whether to have more than one note sounding at a time (by playing on two different strings at once, or what is called *double stops*); among other choices.

These choices may sound like small potatoes, but they're all terribly important to orchestration. For instance, if a violinist plays a melody on the D string, it sounds rather veiled and sweet; but if he plays exactly the same notes, no higher, no lower, but on the G string, it sounds altogether different: fatter and juicier.

All these choices have to be made not only on the violins, but on the other stringed instruments as well. And when several of *these* instruments come together in a family group—as in a string quartet—the choices multiply beyond imagination. The usual string quartet is made up of two violins, a viola and a cello; and a master hand, like Beethoven's, can orchestrate for these four stringed instruments in a way that produces an astonishing number of different-sounding colors.

The great composers were always looking for new, personal sounds, and to get them they wrote for all kinds of different string combinations. Each combination has its own kind of blend. For instance, by adding one more cello to a string quartet—as Schubert does in his *Quintet in C*—a new richness is born. Why did he add a cello, instead of a viola or another violin? Or a double bass? Because he knew that the cello would give him the exact color he needed for that piece of music. That's good orchestration.

Besides quartets and quintets, there are sextets and octets, and there's even a piece for exactly twenty-one strings, by Richard Strauss, called *Metamorphoses*. And so finally we get to a full string orchestra, all the strings

67

you usually see on a concert stage. And it's absolutely amazing, the variety of sounds you can get from an orchestra with nothing but strings in it. The British composer Vaughan Williams gets enormous richness and variety by dividing the string orchestra into two separate half-orchestras, in which the two groups sneak in and out of each other, and change colors like a chameleon. If you ever get a chance, listen to his beautiful work called *Fantasia on a Theme by Tallis.*

On the other hand, there's a completely different way of using a string orchestra—a more rugged, athletic way. The *Symphony for Strings (No. 5)* by William Schuman is an example of this. It has all of Schuman's vitality, American pep, and rugged energy—and it's all done with strings alone!

Now that we've visited the woodwind and string families, let's take a quick look at the other two families in the orchestra community—the brass and the percussion. The brass family isn't very large, compared to the strings, but does it make itself heard!

The members of this family are the trumpets, trombones, the tuba, and, of course, those forty-second cousins (or was it in-laws?) the French horns, who are brass and wind both.

You'd be surprised how many different colors you can get from these brass blockbusters; they don't always have to be just loud and brassy. For instance, there is brass music by an old Italian composer named Gabrieli which sounds something like echoes bouncing off the walls of a cave. Or it can sound organlike, as in the chorale section of Brahms's *First Symphony.* Of course, the brass can also make the more familiar sound, the kind you always hear at a parade, or in a big jazz band.

The percussion family, next door to the brass, is a

whopping big one: it would take a week to name all the percussion instruments, but that's only because almost anything can be a percussion instrument: a frying pan, a baseball bat, a cowbell, or a steam whistle—anything that makes noise. The head of this family is, of course, the tympani, and he's surrounded by all kinds of other drums and bells and clickers and tinklers. But they're a family, too—and there are even pieces orchestrated only for them! (For example, the Mexican composer Carlos Chávez composed a piece in the classical form of the toccata, entirely for percussion instruments.)

So we finally come to the most complicated business of orchestrating for what we call a symphony orchestra. And here's where the family spirit gives way to the friendly social spirit, and the members of the different families begin to mix together. Starting with the smallest combination—two people shyly getting together to see how they get along—we can see the whole story in a nutshell. There are sonatas for flute and piano, for example—two instruments from very different families; but they do get along very nicely indeed. The same is true of a sonata for viola and piano, cello and piano, or flute and harpsichord. In these mixtures there is born a new sound, a new blend. The pure family lines have been broken down, and a new *mixed* musical color emerges.

This social spirit can be enlarged to include, let's say, seven people—as in Ravel's *Introduction and Allegro*, a mixture of harp, flute, clarinet and string quartet. Or you can have an even more mixed-up mixture of seven instruments—such as in Stravinsky's *Story of a Soldier*, where there is a solo violin, a clarinet, a bassoon, a trumpet, a trombone, a double bass, and percussion (one man playing thirteen different percussion instruments!). Now, this begins to be an *orchestral* mixture, because

there is at least one member of every family present: two strings, two winds, two brass and one drummer-boy. It makes a marvelous sound. It's also a great masterpiece that you should try to hear soon.

And so, little by little, we grow up to the regular symphony orchestra we all know. Seven players become seventeen, then seventy, and, finally, one hundred and seven. And you can imagine what a composer must go through to choose from all the possible combinations there are in this mix-up of families. But a good composer always knows, in his heart, what the right choice must be, because if he's good, his music will *make* him choose right. The right music played by the right instruments at the right time in the right combination: that's good orchestration.

It was hard to decide what big piece of music I could recommend for you to listen to that would illustrate all these points—a piece that would show you what *right* orchestration means. I realized that almost any fine piece of music would show this—any symphony of Brahms or Mozart or Beethoven or Berlioz or Tchaikovsky or Stravinsky—and then I thought: What will young people be able to learn from listening to one of these? You would hear beautiful orchestration, but you wouldn't know *why* it was beautiful, unless I took hours and hours, and maybe weeks, to explain it in all its details. Then we'd have to learn to read music, and study each instrument; it would be like a whole course at a conservatory.

So, after much consideration, I've chosen a piece that is perhaps not the greatest example of *composing* in history but is probably the most exciting orchestral exhibition in history: the famous *Bolero* by Ravel.

. . .

71

I recommend the *Bolero* because it's such a marvelously clear example of how a big symphony orchestra can be used. And that's practically *all* it is; it's just one long tune repeated over and over, with the orchestration changing on each repeat, gradually getting bigger and richer and louder until it ends in the biggest orchestral roar you ever heard.

But while it's going on, it gives you a chance to hear the orchestra in all its parts, and with all its special combinations, in a way that no other piece can. The *Bolero* is built up in a very simple way. First of all, there is a bolero dance rhythm that goes on and on, never changing, in the snare drums:

Now over this rhythm that never stops, we hear a tune by the flute:

—a long, smooth, snaky melody, Arabic in feeling— like very aristocratic hootchy-kootchy music. This tune is in two parts, which we'll call Part A and Part B. Part A, which we have just heard from the flute, is repeated, a little richer and fuller, by the clarinet. Now comes Part B, way up high on the bassoon:

Then Part B is repeated on the little E-flat clarinet.

That makes one full section—and that's all the music there is in the whole piece. Over and over again you'll heart Part A twice, followed by Part B twice, then Part A twice again, and so on, always with different instruments, or combinations of instruments, until the whole orchestra has been used up and shown off and has tired itself out. And before it's over, you'll have heard all kinds of delicious sounds, colors and combinations. Each time the orchestration changes, it increases in volume and richness, until by the end everyone gets together in the big roar. It makes an exciting trip through the world of orchestration. Bon voyage, and have a good time when you listen to a recording of *Bolero.*

*W*hat Makes

Music Symphonic?

In the last few years I have found that the audiences at the Young People's Concerts of the New York Philharmonic are the best audiences there are anywhere; that there is nothing young people don't want to learn, or can't understand; that they really want to know about *music*, not just about nice sugar-coated fairy tales that are supposed to make music "easy to take." The response to this kind of one-on-one treatment has warmed my heart, and convinced me that young people find fun in music for its own sake. With this in mind, I have decided to tackle what is perhaps the hardest subject of all: What makes music symphonic?

The reason this is a hard subject is that it has always been *talked* about as a hard subject, using lots of long, hard words. But it's really not so hard, and it's the most exciting part of all music. The key to it is *development*. (See Chapter Eleven on sonata form.) Development is the main thing in music, as it is in life; because development means change, growing, blossoming out, and these things are life itself.

But what does development mean in music? The same thing as in life. A great piece of music has a lifetime of its own between the beginning and the end. In that period all the themes and melodies and musical ideas, however small they are, grow and develop into full-grown works.

How does this happen? How does development work?

It works in three main stages, comparable to infancy, adolescence and maturity. First there is the simple birth, the flower growing out of a little seed. You all know, for example, the seed Beethoven plants at the beginning of his *Fifth Symphony:*

—four little notes, and out of them comes a flower:

Or take Sibelius, the great Finnish composer. He starts *his Fifth Symphony* with another four-note seed:

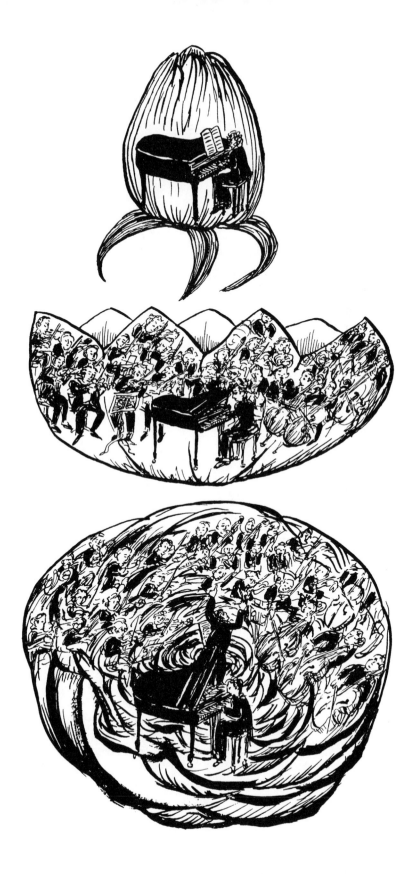

—and before you know it, there's a big shining flower:

Then comes the second stage: the growth of this flower. It gets bigger and bigger with each passing minute. The Beethoven flower a little later on looks like this:

and the Sibelius flower has grown to this:

Then comes the third stage—the most important one: change. The flower actually changes its appearance. Or perhaps it's more like a fruit tree, which we first see bare in winter, then covered with blossoms in the spring; then, in summer, the blossoms fall away and fruit begins to grow. The tree has had three different looks in three seasons; but it's still the same tree.

The same thing happens to us. We change from year to year, in character, in our likes and dislikes, even in our looks. For instance, I was born blond. Could you believe that if you saw me now? And ten years from now I'll probably be completely gray—or bald.[1]

The same thing happens in music.

The Beethoven flower changes in appearance so often and so radically that it becomes almost unrecognizable, as in this example:

where nothing seems to be left of the original theme except the rhythm of those four notes, over and over again.

And the Sibelius flower eventually gets to look like this:

—which is a big change indeed. You see, these themes (whether in the seed stage or in the blossom stage) are played softly, and loudly, and in different keys, and by different instruments; they appear twice as slow, twice as fast, every which way, always changing; but they're always flowers from the same stem. All that is part of the growing-up of a piece, the actual life story of a symphony.

Now, all music isn't symphonic, of course; but all music *does* develop in one way or another, even little folk songs, or a simple popular tune. But those little songs develop mainly by repetition—by saying it over and over again. It's like having an argument; if you're a *good* arguer, you'll develop your argument with variations and changes. Let's say you wanted to prove, just for fun, that Canada is a tropical country. You would try to prove that tropical flowers have been found in Saskatchewan; that on a certain day last winter the sun was hotter in the Canadian Rockies than it was in Miami, etc., etc.

But if you're more babyish and simpleminded, you just say it over and over again: *Canada* is a tropical country, Canada *is* a tropical country, Canada is a *tropical* country.

Well, that's what popular songs do: they develop by beating you over the head.

Take an old tune called "I Want to Be Happy":

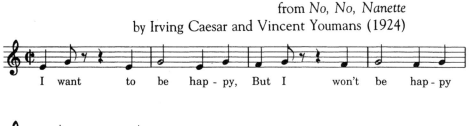

—and then the exact same thing again:

Then follow eight bars which are *somewhat* different; but immediately those first eight bars charge in again, and the song is over.

As we said, repetition is the simplest way of developing music. And the first step toward *real* development is the idea of variation. Now, all variation is a form of repetition, only not *exact* repetition. Something gets changed. That's what makes jazz so exciting: when a jazz player gets hold of a popular song, he doesn't keep repeating it; he makes his own variations on it. (For related discussions see pages 46 and 47, and 107 and 108.) Here's what he might do to "I Want to Be Happy":

Now, that's beginning to be development. It's development because it's changing. But it's not exactly *symphonic* yet. Let's see how Beethoven uses this principle in his *Eroica Symphony*—it's the same idea, but oh, what a difference! In the last movement of this symphony, Beethoven writes a series of variations on a theme that's so skinny and small, it's not even a real tune. It goes like this:

Now, here's how he makes one variation on it, by echoing each of the "skinny" notes an octave higher:

That's one variation. Here's another, with a different and faster tune added to the original notes:

And here's another, in which the new added tune is even faster. But the "skinny" notes remain just as they were:

You see how the original notes are always there no matter what else is going on?

Now look at this next variation, and see those skinny notes in the *bass*, while a beautiful new melody is being played on *top* of them:

You can see what a long way we've come from those first "skinny" notes.

So much for variation. What have we learned so far? That all music, to some degree or other, depends on development; and the more it develops, the more symphonic it is. *And* that the basis of all development is repetition, but the less exact the repetition is, the more symphonic it is, also. So what we have to find out now is: How do composers use repetition in a *not-exact* way, to develop their themes into big symphonic pieces?

The first way, we've already seen—variation. But there's another way, just as common; in fact I'd say that there's hardly a standard symphonic piece played that doesn't use this device—and that is *sequences*.

It's a very simple trick, really. All a sequence does is to repeat any series of notes at a different pitch. That's all. For instance, I could make a sequence out of almost anything—like that old Elvis Presley number "All Shook Up":

That's a sequence. You can see right away how useful it is in developing music; because it's a way of building—like piling up bricks—higher and higher, and that gives the impression of going somewhere: in other words, a development.

Of course, a sequence can also repeat at lower pitches—but that's not so widely used, because it's not half so exciting, and doesn't keep mounting up.

Let's look at some examples of sequences in symphonic music. Here's one of the most famous sequences in history—from Tchaikovsky's *Romeo and Juliet*; and just see how this love music builds up:

Do you recognize those sequences, piling up power until the music explodes like dynamite?

As you see, sequences are a very easy way to develop

music; it's a form of climbing repetition that's almost guaranteed to sound exciting. Look how Gershwin uses them in his *Rhapsody in Blue.* You remember this theme from it?

Well, here's how he develops it by sequences:

But that's enough about sequences. There's still a much more important way in which repetition works for development, and that is something called *imitation*—the imitation of one orchestral voice by another.

Now, why is this different from any other kind of repetition? Is it just because a phrase is played first by an oboe and then imitated by the violins, or vice versa? No, not at all. The exciting thing about imitation is that when the second voice comes in, imitating the first, the first voice goes on playing something else, so that there are suddenly *two* melodies happening at once, as you will see in our discussion of the Bach Erector Set (see pages 113–17). That's the great musical device called *counterpoint*—more than one melody at a time. You sing counterpoint yourself—every time you sing a round like "Row, Row, Row Your Boat," or *"Frère Jacques,"* or "Three Blind Mice." But I would like you to think of these rounds with *imitation* in mind, so that you can see how symphonic music develops in the same way.

For instance, your sister starts singing "Three Blind Mice," and when she gets to the words "See how they run," your father comes in with the opening tune. And when she reaches "They all ran after the farmer's wife," your father is up to "See how they run," while *you* begin at the beginning with "Three blind mice." Now you have real imitation.

What we have just been talking about is, in musical language, a canon. And a canon can get very rich and complicated, depending on how many imitating voices there are. And it can get, of course, even more complicated when it becomes a fugue, as we will see with the Bach Erector Set.

All we have to know is this: that in developments that use canons and fugues the greatest changes of all can happen to musical themes. For instance, the theme can turn up twice as slow, or twice as fast. And it can also appear backwards and upside down. These are all ways of using imitation and counterpoint to change the shape of music so as to give it new life all the time. It's like looking at musical material from every possible angle,

over and under and from all sides, until you know everything about it there is to know. Then you can really say, "I've seen this material *developed.*"

All these ways we've been talking about are ways of building up—developing themes by adding to them, adding voices, adding sequences, adding variation or decoration. But there is also a way of developing that builds up by *breaking down*—now, doesn't that sound very peculiar? But it's true, and a very good method it is, too. It was a great favorite of Beethoven's, and also of Tchaikovsky's. In his *Fourth Symphony*, for example, Tchaikovsky is developing this phrase:

And, as usual, he treats it first in sequences:

But now, instead of adding to it, he builds excitement by breaking it in half, and using only the second half of it, again in sequences:

Then he breaks *that* in half and develops just the second half—now down to four notes only, but still in sequences:

But now it divides again, like an amoeba, and the sequence builds on the last *two* notes only:

Finally it's broken down to such tiny fragments that it's just dust, ashes, whirling scales:

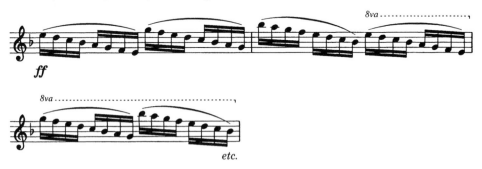

etc.

What excitement and fury Tchaikovsky *builds up* by *breaking down!* This is, strange as it sounds, making music grow by destroying it.

I think that we've seen enough ways in which music can grow and change and blossom so that we're ready now to take a good look at a whole movement of a symphony, and see how it develops, bit by bit. Then, after we analyze some of it, I think you'll be able to hear it in a brand-new way—not just as a bunch of tunes, or exciting sounds by a big orchestra, but as a whole process of growing, which is the most important thing to be able to hear in any piece of music. Then—but not before you read the next few pages—play a recording of Brahms's *Second Symphony.*

We're going to put the last movement of this symphony by Brahms under our microscope. It is brilliant, joyful, satisfying music. What makes it so satisfying is the way

it develops. It starts right off with the main theme, a long, lyrical melody:

Now, there are certain elements in that softly whispered melody that are going to come in for a lot of changes: the opening figure—

—which is really two different elements; this—

—and this:

Then there is this phrase, which is made up of descending intervals of fourths:

But then, a few bars later, these same fourths are used again, in another rhythm:

You see how it's *already* begun to develop, even while the melody is still being played for the first time. These fourths:

have turned into:

—and that's already a big rhythmic change, a growth, a development. Then immediately this figure, which the strings have been playing, is repeated by the woodwinds. So there's another development—of orchestral color.

The next change is what we call a dynamic change—
a change in loudness. The same melody is now repeated
much more loudly. A simple change, from whispering to
shouting, but that's also a development.

Now, after a few more bars, we run into something
new called *augmentation,* which is only a long word for
our old friend *Twice-as-slow.* All it means is that you
take the notes of your melody and spread them out more
thinly, so that they take up more room; and that's a great
way of developing your melody. That's what Brahms does
here. He takes those fourths we spoke of before:

and spreads them out this way:

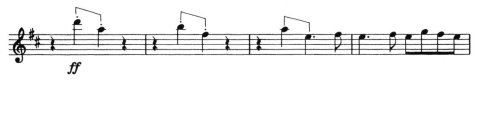

You see how this bigger way of saying the same thing
actually changes the shape of the tune? It's a solid
rhythmic change. We're really moving now.

At this very point, Brahms uses the old standby, sequence. And the sequences are built on the very last
measure we just spoke of:

95

Here it goes building up its power:

etc.

Now, here's something amazing: At the top of this mounting sequence, Brahms is developing not only the notes of the sequence, but—at the same time—that first figure from the very beginning of the piece:

etc.

And he's doing it by taking those notes and squeezing them together like an accordion so that they take up *less* room instead of more—just the opposite of what he did before, when he spread them out:

This squeezing together, or making the notes smaller, is called *diminution*, the opposite of augmentation, and you can just forget both of these words right here and now.

I don't care if you *ever* remember words like augmentation and diminution, or any other words, for that matter, as long as you remember the musical purpose they describe—the making bigger and the making smaller—which are so necessary to developing music.

Well, that's a lot of development so far, but there's no end to the tricks Brahms has for making his music grow. For instance, at this point, where we just left off, he takes the squeezed-together notes and turns them into an accompaniment playing *under* a new, sweet melody, which is itself an augmentation—development of those fourths we heard before. Only now the fourths are twice as slow:

Whenever I hear this part, I am always filled with wonder and respect for the way Brahms makes everything in his music out of something else in his music. It's all part of one great thought, and every single part is a branch of the same great tree.

Now Brahms is ready to give us his second theme, a rich, broad, beautiful melody:

But even here, in a brand-new melody, Brahms works in a development of something earlier: He takes the opening notes of the movement:

and makes a figure out of them that moves along under the melody:

connecting it to what we've heard before, like connecting a new branch to the tree:

Next, this new melody comes in for a change—this time by changing from what is called the major, which is how we've just seen this theme, to the minor; and this development takes place:

98

This minor version of the second theme carries us back to our opening theme, only now in a whole new rhythmic dress:

and developed even more by a simple scale, going down:

As this development goes on, the scales become more and more important, until there's nothing *but* scales, going down and up, and every which way.

Now, this may sound absolutely crazy to you, but the truth is that Brahms has not yet even reached what is usually called the development section of this movement. Can you imagine that? He still has before him the *main* job of developing, but his mind was so musical, so full of musical ideas, that he couldn't even write out his simple *melodies* without developing them at the same time. That's why in this short first part of the movement he has already developed more than most composers do in a whole symphony.

If we had the space, I'd love to go through the rest of this amazing movement, and show you all the other marvelous ways in which he grows his music, like a master gardener: the way he uses variation, and puts two and three melodies together in counterpoint; the way he uses that breaking-up system we talked about before; the way he takes little scraps of his melodies and develops them by themselves; and the way he turns themes upside down, as in this place, which is that old first theme—

—just turned over like a pancake.

But the remarkable thing is not just that the melody is upside down; it's the fact that it's upside down, and *sounds wonderful* upside down. You see, anyone can take a tune and turn it upside down, or play it backwards, or twice as fast, or twice as slow—but the question is: Will it be beautiful? That's what makes Brahms so great; the music doesn't just change, it changes beautifully.

The trick is not just to use all these different ways of developing, but to use them when it's right to use them, so that the music always makes sense as music, as *expression*. That's hard to do, and that's what Brahms could do as ingeniously and beautifully as any composer who ever lived.

So now that you have some idea of what makes music symphonic—and the answer, as you know very well by now, is *development*—I hope you won't stop here, but will go on and actually listen to this music we've been talking about. I'm also hoping that now you'll be able to hear it with new ears, able to hear the *symphonic* wonders of it, the growth of it, the miracle of life that runs like blood through its veins, that connects very note to every other note, making it the great music it is.

*W*hat Is Classical Music?

 The question before the house is: What is Classical Music? Now, anybody knows Handel wrote classical music, and it sounds classical, too. You can tell it right away—even from just four bars, like these, from his *Water Music:*

Right? So what's the problem? Why are we asking this question? Well, there's a good reason, as we're going to find out.

Almost everybody *thinks* he knows what classical music is: just any music that isn't jazz, like a Tijuana Brass arrangement; or a popular song, like "I Can't Give You Anything But Love"; or folk music, like an African war dance or "Twinkle, Twinkle, Little Star." But that's no way to say what classical music *is*. You can't define it by saying what it *isn't*.

People use the word "classical" to describe music that isn't jazz or pop songs or folk music, just because there isn't any other word that seems to describe it better.

All the other words that are used are just as wrong, like "good" music for instance. You've heard people say, "I just love good music"—meaning Handel instead of Bob Dylan.[1] You know what they mean, but after all, isn't there such a thing as *good* jazz, or a *good* pop song? So you can't use the word "good" to describe just one kind of music. There's good Handel and good Bob Dylan; and so we'll have to forget *that* word.

Then people use the words "serious music" when they mean Handel or Beethoven, but there again, there's some jazz that's very serious, and heavens—what's more serious than an African war dance? So that word's no good either.

Some people use the word "highbrow," which means that only very smart, well-educated people can understand and like it. But we know that's wrong, because we all know a lot of people who aren't exactly Einsteins who will—to use "lowbrow" talk—dig Beethoven the most.

What about calling it "art" music then? A lot of people use that word to try to describe the difference between Beethoven and Dave Brubeck. But that's no good either, because just as many other people think that jazz is also an art—which indeed it is.

And if we try to use the word "symphony" music—well, that leaves out all the music written for piano solo, violin solo and string quartet. Certainly that's all supposed to be classical, too, isn't it?

Maybe the best word invented so far is, of all things,

"longhair," because it was made up by jazz musicians themselves to nail down all the music that isn't theirs. But we've seen enough jazz musicians and rock stars with long hair on their own heads, so I guess even that word won't do.

Since, then, all those words are wrong, let's try to find one that's right by finding out first what the real difference is between the different kinds of music.

The real difference is that when a composer writes a piece of what's usually called classical music, he puts down the exact notes that he wants, the exact instruments or voices that he wants to play or sing them— even to the exact *number* of instruments or voices. He also writes down as many directions as he can think of, to tell the players or singers as carefully as he can everything they need to know about how fast or slow it should go, how loud or soft it should be, and millions of other things to help the performers give an *exact* performance of those notes he thought up. Of course, no performance can be perfectly exact, for there aren't enough words in the world to tell the performers everything they have to know about what the composer wanted. But that's just what makes the performer's job so exciting—to try to figure out, from what the composer *did* write down, as exactly as possible what he wanted.

Now, of course, performers are only human, and so each one always figures it out a little differently. For instance, one conductor will decide that the beginning of Beethoven's *Fifth Symphony*[2]—which I'm sure you know—

—should get a big extra bang on that last long note, like this:

Another conductor, who is trying just as hard as the first one to figure out what Beethoven wanted, might feel that it's the *first* note of the four that should get the strongest accent. Like this:

Then still another conductor—maybe not so faithful to Beethoven as the first two—might decide that the four notes should be played very importantly, slower and more majestic. Like this:

But in spite of these differences, which come out of the different personalities of these three conductors, they're still all conducting the same notes, in the same rhythm (though not necessarily in the same tempo), with the same instruments, and with the same purpose: to make Beethoven's printed notes come to life in the way they think he'd want them to. This means that what people call classical music can't be changed, except by

the personality of the performer. This music is perma-
nent, unchangeable, exact. There's a good word: *exact*—
maybe that's what we should call this kind of music:
exact music. Within limits, there's only one way it can
be played, and that way has been told us by the composer
himself.

But if we take a popular song, like "I Can't Give You
Anything But Love, Baby," there's no end to the ways
in which it can be played. It can be sung by a chorus,
or by Louis Armstrong, or by Maria Callas, or by nobody
at all. It can just be *played* without words by a jazz band
or a symphony orchestra or a kazoo, slow or fast, hot or
sentimental, loud or soft. It doesn't matter. It can be
played through once or repeated fifteen times, in any
key, even with the chords underneath changed. Even
the tune itself can be changed and improvised on and
fooled around with.

For instance, the way the tune goes on the printed sheet
is like this:

But when Louis Armstrong sings it, it goes something
like this:

107

or when a cool, progressive cat plays it on the piano, it might sound something like this:

or if it were sung by the Fred Waring Glee Club it would have a completely different sound. Something like this:

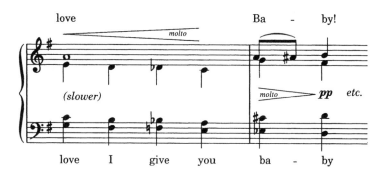

But the main thing about all this is that none of these ways is *wrong*. Each way seems right for those particular performers who are doing it at the time, and right for the particular occasion at which they're doing it—as, for instance, for dancing, or at Birdland, or for a television show. There isn't any one way that this song has to be done, which means that it's not *exact* music. It doesn't have to be done exactly the same way the composer wrote it. In fact, what's even more important is that popular songs definitely should *not* be played the way the composer wrote them, the same way all the time. Just imagine how deadly dull it would be if the only way you ever heard "I Can't Give You Anything But Love" was the way the sheet music reads!

The same thing goes for folk music too. It can and should change with every performer. Of course, there's even more reason for changing folk music, because no composer laid down the law about how it should go. And as far as jazz is concerned, of course, it changes all the time, because that's what jazz is all about. It's improvising—making the music up as you go along, and never bothering to write it down.

So now at least we have a better word for classical music: *exact* music. And while there may be an even better word for it (which I can't think of at the moment), at least it's not a wrong word; and classical *is* a wrong word.

Why is the word classical a wrong word? Because, you see, while it's true that there *is* such a thing as classical music, it means something very different from what we've been talking about. It doesn't mean longhair music; it means only one certain *kind* of longhair music. For instance, take this well-known musical phrase from Rimsky-Korsakoff's *Scheherazade:*

Is that classical music? If you answer yes, you're wrong. Classical music refers to a very definite period of the history of music, which is called the *classical* period. The

music that was written in that time is called classical
music, and *Scheherazade* simply wasn't written in that
time. But *this* music, by Mozart, *was:*

I'm sure you can tell the difference between *Scheherazade*
and this theme from a piano concerto by Mozart. The
Mozart is classical music; the *Scheherazade* is not.

Now let's get some idea of what this classical period
was like. It lasted about a hundred years, from about

1700 to 1800. What do we know about this eighteenth century? Well, let's take the first fifty years of it.[3] We all know what America was like during those years. It was still being settled; pioneers were exploring new savage territories; there were new frontiers; we were fighting Indians. In other words, we were going through a tough time, living a rough life and building a new country from the ground up.

This same time in Europe was very different. Over there we find a nice old civilization that had been building for hundreds of years; and so by the time the eighteenth century rolled around, Europe was no longer just exploring and nailing logs together. It was trying to make perfect what it had already built. These same first fifty years in Europe were a time of rules and regulations, and of getting those rules and regulations to be as exactly right as possible.

This is what makes classicism—this bringing of rules to a pitch of perfection. It makes classical architecture, classical drama and classical music. That's what classical music really means: music written in a time when perfect form and balance are what everybody is looking for, music which tries more than anything else to have a perfect shape—like the shape of a beautiful vase.

The two giant musical names of these first fifty years of the eighteenth century were Bach and Handel. Especially Bach, because he took all the rules that the composers who lived before him had been experimenting with, and fiddling with, and made those rules as perfect as a human being can make them.

For instance, take the form called the fugue. People had been writing various kinds of fugues for a long time before Bach; but once Bach got hold of this form, he made it better than it had ever been. He made a classical form out of it, by getting its rules and regulations perfectly organized, once and for all, for all time.

The rules of a fugue are something like the printed directions you get when you buy an Erector Set. They tell you exactly how to build a house, or a fire truck, or

a Ferris wheel. You start the Ferris wheel by attaching one metal section to another on the floor; then you add one exactly four notches higher; then another one five notches higher than that, and so on. Then you make the wheel that goes around the whole construction.

That's just what Bach does in a fugue. Take this one, for instance, from his *Fourth Brandenburg Concerto.* He lays the foundation for his Ferris wheel by starting first with the theme in the viola—that's the first section:

Then he adds the second section—by a violin, exactly four notches higher—which means, in musical words, four notes higher[4] (and, in this case, four measures later):

Then the third piece is attached, by another violin, *five* notches higher (and again four measures later):

Then the fourth piece, by the cello and bass, this time way down underneath:

And finally, the fifth piece is fitted into place, by the flute, way up on top:

Now the foundation is built, and Bach can start surrounding it with the big wheel. The wonderful thing about that foundation is that it's not just five separate bits, one at a time. They're all joined together; which means that whenever a new instrument is added, playing the theme, the others still go on playing something else; so that by the time the fifth piece is attached—by the flute—you have five different parts all going at once—just as the five different pieces of the Erector Set are all joined together at once.

Turn the page and you will see it all together:

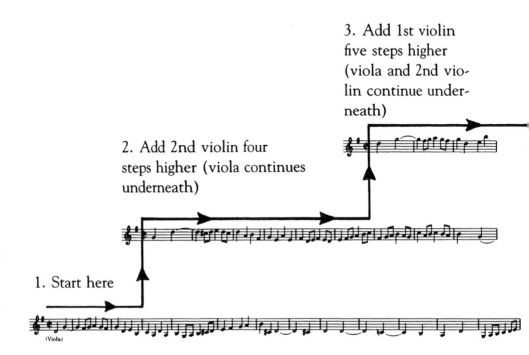

3. Add 1st violin
five steps higher
(viola and 2nd vio-
lin continue under-
neath)

2. Add 2nd violin four
steps higher (viola continues
underneath)

1. Start here

(Viola)

5. Finally, on top, add flute.

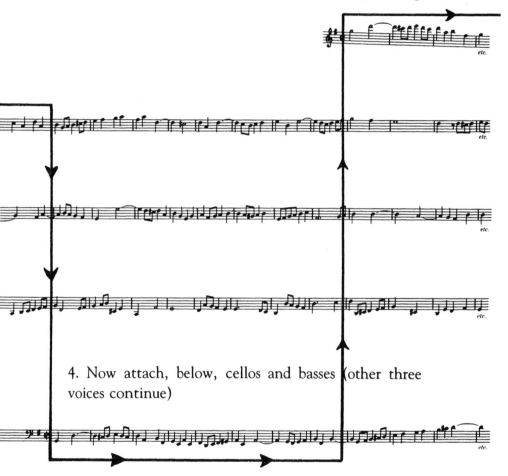

4. Now attach, below, cellos and basses (other three voices continue)

Isn't that a marvelous structure?[5] That is classical perfection.

Now, Bach died in 1750, which is very convenient
for us, because it just neatly divides the eighteenth century in half. The next fifty years were very different indeed. Everything changed; the new big giants were
Haydn and Mozart, and their music is completely different from Bach's. It was still classical music, because
Haydn and Mozart were still looking for the same thing
Bach was looking for—perfection of form and shape. But
not through fugues any more—it was going to be a different story now.

How does such a change happen? Do composers just
go to a convention, like a political or a business con-
vention in a big hotel, and decide by voting to change

the style of music? Not at all. It happens by itself, for as times change, and history changes, people change. Composers are people too, so it stands to reason that their music is also going to change.

The people of Haydn and Mozart's time thought Bach was old-fashioned and boring with all his serious fugues and things. They wanted something new—not so complicated—with pretty tunes and easy accompaniments, music that was elegant and refined and pleasant. And this was right in line with the times: a time of elegance and refinement, good manners, proper etiquette; a time of lace cuffs and silk suits, powdered wigs and jeweled fans, for the ladies and gentlement of the court. So out came lovely, elegant music for them in which the main thing was the tune. Take this marvelous tune from that same piano concerto by Mozart we spoke of before, for instance. There's no Erector Set here; only the gorgeous melody, with a simple little accompaniment underneath—simple, but oh, how beautiful!

Nobody could write melodies like Mozart. But that melody is also full of rules and regulations, just as Bach's
fugue was; only there are a great many other rules, rules
which make the easy, pleasant kind of music that was
wanted in those second fifty years of the century.

Another thing about this new, easy, pleasant kind of
music was that it was fun. Those people in lace cuffs and
powdered wigs wanted to be entertained. They wanted
amusement and pleasure out of music—beautiful melo-

120

dies, yes—but also gay, witty, high spirits. Mozart was a master of *this,* too. For instance, the overture to Mozart's opera *The Marriage of Figaro* is a very strict piece that follows still another set of rules about something called sonata form, which we won't go into now (but read Chapter Eleven on sonata form)—but it's as different from a Bach fugue as milk is from orange juice. The main thing about it is not how it's put together, like that old Erector Set, but that it's gay and witty and exciting— and fun. It's like a ride in a roller coaster, full of laughing and good humor. It makes you have a good time; it makes you smile.

But when it comes to humor in music—real jokes—
nobody beats Haydn. He was the great master of amusement. Now, there's one thing you should know about
jokes in music: you can't make a musical joke about
anything except music. Which doesn't mean music can't
be funny; it's only that it can't be funny about "two
Martians landed on the Earth and said, 'Take us to your
leader' " or "There were three Scotchmen sitting on a
fence." E-flats and F-sharps can't tell you anything about
Martians and Scotchmen, but they still can make you
laugh—and the way they do it is by surprising you. Surprise is one of the main ways to make anyone laugh, like
sneaking up behind someone and yelling "Boo!" or by
April Fool jokes, or by saying hello to someone who is
expecting you to say goodbye.

In music, composers can make these surprises in lots
of different ways: by making the music loud when you
expect it to be soft, or the other way around; or by
suddenly stopping in the middle of a phrase; or by writing
a wrong note on purpose, a note you don't expect, that
doesn't belong to the music. Let's try one, just for fun.
You all know those silly notes that go:

Shave and a hair - cut,   two   bits!

Now you sing "Shave and a haircut," then play two wrong
notes on the piano for "two bits," and see what happens:
You sing:

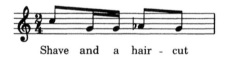

Shave and a hair - cut

122

Now play these notes:

ff

You see? It's a shock, and so it's funny. But you probably didn't laugh out loud. Most people don't laugh out loud about musical jokes. That's one of the things about musical humor: you laugh *inside.* Otherwise you could never listen to a Haydn symphony—the laughter would drown out the music. But that doesn't mean a Haydn symphony isn't funny. You've heard his *Surprise Symphony* over and over again, where he suddenly bangs out a loud chord in the middle of a soft little piece. But Haydn can also make you laugh in a hundred other ways. The last movement of his *B-flat symphony—No. 102*—(Imagine writing 102 symphonies, and, in fact, he wrote 104!)—anyway, this last movement of *No. 102* is full of

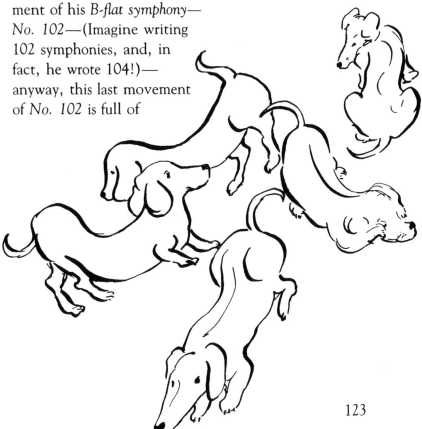

123

surprises and fun. Let me show you some of the ways Haydn makes fun in this piece.

It starts with this tune, which is fast and gay, and skitters all over the place like a funny little dachshund puppy:

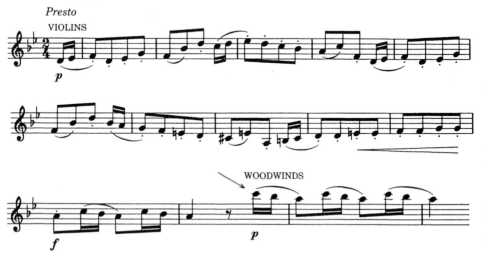

That last little echo in the woodwinds is like someone laughing at something you just said. If you say very seriously:

and someone makes fun of you, and goes:

you may not like him for doing it, but it's still fun; it's like teasing. That's just what Haydn does: the serious old strings have their say, and the little piping woodwinds make fun of them, by imitating and mocking.

124

Then, later on, after he's been through some other
tunes and jokes, he has to come back to his first tune
we just mentioned. And the way he slips into it is again
a surprise. He just sneaks back to it, when you least expect
it—as though you thought your kid brother had gone
away on a trip, and suddenly there he is, hiding under
the kitchen table. Here's how Haydn does it:

You see how sneakily he got back to it: while you weren't
looking—*boom,* and he's there.

Later on he sneaks back again, but in a different way—
as though your kid brother now suddenly turned up in
the bathtub:

There are lots of other musical jokes in this movement.
Like this one—where Haydn pretends to be starting the
tune again, and then surprises you by not doing it at all.

125

Pretending is always fun. It's like a trick: I have a penny in my hand—whoosh, where did it go? That's what Haydn does:

And how about that last loud scale? That was really like yelling "Boo!" Then he goes on making more false starts, scaring you with more sudden louds and sudden softs:

This whole movement is not very long, but funny things shouldn't be long anyway. Haven't you always noticed that the shorter a joke is, the more you laugh? We all know people who tell jokes badly, and that's usually because they don't get to the punch line soon enough. Well, Haydn does; he's the best joke-teller in the history of music. The subject of humor in music is, in fact, so interesting that I am going to devote the entire next chapter to it.

Of course, that doesn't mean that *all* classical music is supposed to be funny. It can be very serious. All I'm saying is that wit and humor are one important part of

126

this music of Haydn and Mozart, along with elegance, grace, and supple strength.

But most of all it has *classic* beauty. It sets up its rules of balance and form just as strictly as Bach did in his fugues. It is looking for perfection.

Now, you may say: if that was the most important thing—perfect form, rules and so on—then where does emotion come in? People always think that feeling and emotion are the main thing in music. It should make you *feel* something—not just laughter—but sorrow or pain or victory or spiritual joy exactly as I said in our very first program, "What Does Music Mean?". The fact is that Mozart and Haydn *do* make you feel all these things, even using strict rules and being so much interested in proportions and shapes. Any great composer, writing music in any period, classical or not classical, will make you feel deep emotions, because he's great—because he has something to say, something to tell you in his music. And that's why a great composer's music will always last and last, perhaps forever, because people keep on feeling emotions whenever they hear it. And that lasting quality is perhaps the most important meaning of the word "classical."

A classic is something that lasts forever, like a Greek vase, or Robinson Crusoe, or Shakespeare's plays, or a Mozart symphony. There were hundreds of classical composers writing at the time of Mozart—writing fine pieces, that stuck to all the rules, and were elegant and proper and all the rest of it. But their music doesn't last, for it just doesn't make the people who hear it feel something— feel the sense of classical perfection, with that extra something added.

And that extra something is what we call beauty; and what we call beauty has to do with our feelings. That's what Mozart's music has—beauty. For instance, when we listen to that gorgeous melody from his concerto quoted earlier, we are moved and touched—we *feel* something. Listening to that long, wonderful line of notes, you feel deep feelings—almost sad, but not quite, and yet not really happy. They are very special feelings:

etc.

Now, the classical period we've been talking about came to an end in the beginning of the nineteenth century, with Beethoven. Most people think of him as the greatest composer of all time. Why should this be? Because Beethoven took all those classical rules of Mozart and Haydn and stretched them till his music got bigger in every way. Where Haydn made a sweet little joke, to be told in a living room, Beethoven makes jokes that are world-shaking, to be told in the middle of a raging storm. Where Haydn made amusing surprises, Beethoven makes astonishing surprises that leave you gasping, not smiling.[6] Where Mozart was gay, Beethoven is crazy with joy. It's like looking at classical music through a magnifying glass—it's all much bigger. But the main thing Beethoven added to classical music was much more personal emotion. His emotions are bigger, and easier to see.

We call that *romanticism*; and that's the name we give to the music written in the hundred years after Beethoven. It means being very free with your emotions,

128

not so reserved and proper and shy, but telling your deepest feelings without even thinking whether you should or not.

Let's see if I can give you an example. If I'm introduced to a girl named Miss Smith, and I say, "How do you do, Miss Smith, I'm very happy to make your acquaintance"—then I'm being classical: proper, elegant, refined—obeying the rules.

But if I say, "How do you do, what gorgeous eyes you have, I love you"—then I'm being a romantic. I'm expressing my feelings right away, unashamed. I'm full of fire and passion, and I don't care who knows it.

See if you can feel that in this music of Chopin, for example, who was a real romantic:

REVOLUTIONARY ÉTUDE, OP. 10, NO. 12

Or listen to this by the great romantic composer Schumann:

Now again, the romantic composers didn't just hold a convention in Chicago and vote to go romantic. Again it's a reflection of changes that happen in history, in the way people live and think and feel and act. And it all began, strangely enough, with that greatest classicist of all, Beethoven.

He was two things in one, you see—the last man of the classical period, and the first man of the romantic period.[7] I guess you could say that he was a classicist who went too far. He was so full of feeling and emotion that he couldn't keep himself chained up in all those rules and regulations of the eighteenth century. And so he just broke his chains, and started a whole new kind of music. And that was the end of classical music.

So what have we learned? First, that classical music does *not* mean just longhair music, but certain special

130

kinds of longhair music that were written in the eighteenth century, by Bach and Handel, then by Mozart and Haydn, and finally by the great Beethoven. Beethoven's *Egmont Overture,* for example, is as classical as you can get, and yet it is full of romantic feelings—like mystery, longing, rage, triumph and joy. Of course, it's not yet the big, wild kind of romanticism that will come later in the music of Chopin and Schumann, and Tchaikovsky and Wagner and the rest. Beethoven is the *beginning* of romantic music. Don't forget that he still comes out of the eighteenth century, even though he lived over a quarter of a century into the nineteenth; and that his rules, even though he breaks them, are still classical rules. He was still trying to perfect these rules; and in the best of his music he came as close to perfection as any human being has since the world began.

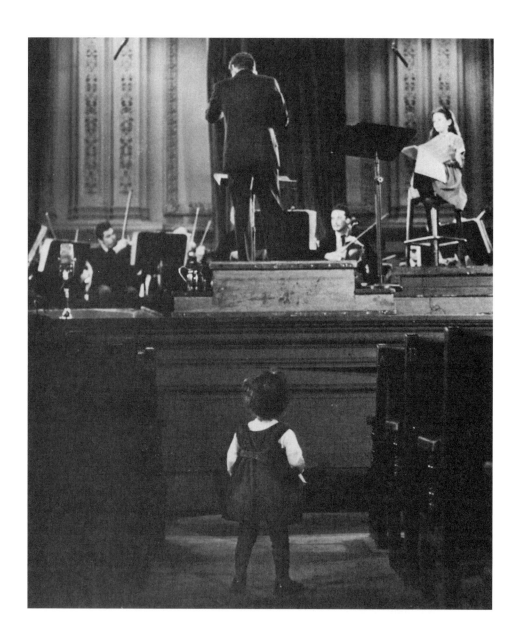

$\mathcal{H}$umor in Music

What makes music funny? That's an easier question to ask than to answer. The main trouble seems to be that the minute you explain why something is funny, it isn't funny any more. For instance, take a joke—any joke, like this shaggy old story: An elephant was making fun of a mouse because he was so tiny. The elephant said, "Huh, look at you, you little peanut, you shrimp, you're not even as big as my left toenail!" And the mouse said, "Listen, I've been sick!"

Well, what's so funny about that? It always gets a laugh; and we can perhaps explain why: because the answer is so unexpected and shocking. There has to be that element of surprise and shock in every joke—the thing that's called the twist, or the gimmick, or the punch, or the topper, or the tag line; but whatever you call it, it's got to be a surprise, a shock, and that's what makes you laugh. Who would have expected that the mouse would try to excuse his smallness by saying that he's been sick? But once we explain that fact, you don't laugh any more; the joke may have been funny, but the explanation isn't. As I said earlier, we all know people who insist on telling you a joke and then explaining to you why it's funny. There's nothing worse. They just kill the joke.

The other trouble with trying to explain humor is that it's such a big subject—there are so many different kinds of humor: like wit, satire, parody, caricature, burlesque, or just plain clowning around.

All these different kinds of humor can be found in music too. But there's one very important thing we have to know about humor in *music*: it's got to be funny for musical reasons. Music can't make jokes about anything except music itself; it can make fun of itself, or of other pieces of music, but it can never make jokes about an elephant and a mouse.

Yet when music is funny, it's funny in the same way that a joke is funny. It does something shocking, surprising, unexpected, absurd. It puts two things together that don't belong together, things which are *incongruous*. Thus Alice, when she gets all mixed up in the strange new world of Wonderland, and can't remember anything right, seems to hear the Mad Hatter reciting:

> *Twinkle, twinkle, little bat!*
> *How I wonder what you're at!*
> *Up above the world you fly,*
> *Like a tea-tray in the sky.*

Incongruous? Yes, because tea-trays just have nothing to do with the sky, or with bats either. Incongruous things don't make *sense*, so we get *non-sense*—and nonsense is the loveliest thing there is. It makes us laugh.

134

Of course, some music does make certain jokes that aren't about music; but then they're not *musical* jokes. For instance, in a ballet called *The Incredible Flutist* by the American composer Walter Piston, there is a part imitating a parade. There are two things which make this section funny. First, we have a symphony orchestra imitating a brass marching band. That's incongruous. The second is the fact that everyone in the orchestra begins cheering and yelling just as people do at a parade. That's *incongruous*, too. But that yelling isn't *music*; so it's not funny for *musical* reasons.

It's the same with a little piece called "Mosquito Dance" by another American, Paul White: the big laugh comes when the mosquito gets slapped by the use of a slapstick. But that, again, isn't music; it's a noise, but not a *musical* noise. And the same is true, once more, of the taxi horns you hear in Gershwin's *An American in Paris*: they give you an amusing idea of Paris, with its millions of cars and taxis rushing around and honking away, but they're a separate thing from the music. They're just noise and not music.[1]

That's enough about musical jokes that *aren't* musical. Now let's look at music that has humor in it without using slaps and horns and yelling—music that makes its jokes with notes, plain old musical notes.

The first and simplest way that music can be amusing is by simply imitating nature. That's one of the oldest ways of making you laugh—imitating things or people. It's like comedians who do impersonations of famous stars: like imitating Greta Garbo ("I vahnt to be alone") or Katharine Hepburn ("Oh, it's LAHVly, just LAHVly"). But the way music does this is by imitating sounds—sounds we all know, like mosquitoes, or trains, or oxcarts, or little chickens, or even a big sneeze.

For instance, there is a great musical sneeze that the Hungarian composer Zoltán Kodály wrote in his suite called *Háry János*. It winds up slowly, like heavy breathing, and then explodes—*chaa!*—in fifty directions.

This business of imitating goes way back to the earliest composers, like the old Frenchman, Rameau, who wrote all kinds of pieces for the harpsichord imitating cuckoo birds, and roosters, and what not. Here's one that imitates a hen going "*co-co-co-co-co-co-co-dai*":

co - co - co - co - co - co-co-dai *etc.*

But let's not get too involved with imitations. Let's get down to the real heart of the matter: wit. As you will recall, we've already discussed this aspect of humor in connection with a symphony by Haydn. I am sure you noticed his wit: how he surprised you all the time; how he got fun into the music through sudden pauses, sudden louds and softs; and how he made humor through using

those fast, scurrying themes that remind us of a little dachshund puppy skittering around the floor. You might read through pages 123 to 126 again, just to refresh your memory and have some fun. For one of the great things about purely musical jokes it that, unlike most jokes that you tell, they are even better fun as they grow more familiar.

And how fast that Haydn movement flies by! Speed has always been one of the main things about wit; fast and funny—that's the rule for jokes. That's why those tongue-twister songs of Gilbert and Sullivan are so funny—they go at such an impossible speed. Like this one from the *Pirates of Penzance*:

MAJOR-GENERAL'S SONG

I am the very model of a modern Major-Gineral,
I've information vegetable, animal, and mineral,
I know the kings of England, and I quote the fights
    historical,
From Marathon to Waterloo, in order categorical;
I'm very well acquainted too with matters mathematical,
I understand equations, both the simple and quadratical,
About binomial theorem I'm teeming with a lot
    o'news—
With many cheerful facts about the square of the
    hypotenuse.

(Try singing this. Or, if you don't know the tune, just read it—four lines to a breath, and spitting out each syllable with equal emphasis. The faster you do this, as you see, the funnier it becomes.)

Haydn does the same thing. He used speed to get humorous effect. In that finale of his *Symphony No. 102*, this same sort of breathless excitement can be heard.

While it won't make you laugh out loud, I think you see what I mean when I call it witty. It's like a bag full of magic tricks coming at you so fast you can almost not follow them.

Now we come to a new department of humor, called satire. This is in itself a pretty big department. Satire includes all those other words like "parody," "caricature," "burlesque," and so on. They all mean roughly the same thing—making fun of something by exaggerating it or twisting it in some way. But still, there's a difference between "satire" and the other words. Satire makes fun of things in order to say something new, and possibly even beautiful; in other words, it has a real purpose of its own. But parody, for instance, makes fun of things just for the fun of making fun of them. This will be clearer when you hear music that shows the difference.

For instance, one of the best musical satires ever written is by the modern Russian composer Prokofieff. It's his *Classical Symphony*. (See also Chapter Eleven, pages 242–43.) This is a perfect jewel of a symphony, an out-and-out imitation of Haydn. In form it is just like a Haydn symphony, only it exaggerates the surprises, the sudden louds and softs, the stops and pauses, the elegant tunes, and all the rest. And every so often something very peculiar sneaks in—a little wrong note, or one beat too many, or one beat too few; and then it goes right on again, deadpan, as though nothing at all strange has happened.

It's this combination of exaggerating, which is always funny, plus the little hints of modern music that keep popping up—which is *incongruous* in this eighteenth-century type of piece. It's that combination that makes it funny.

I think this is the only piece of music I ever laughed

at out loud. I still remember the first time I heard it, on the radio when I was about fifteen years old. I remember lying on the floor and laughing till I cried. I didn't know what the piece was. I'd never heard of Prokofieff. I only knew that there was something very peculiar and funny and beautiful going on.

For instance, in the third movement of this symphony, Prokofieff provides us with a delicious gavotte—a gavotte being an elegant eighteenth-century dance. And the satire here is in the way Prokofieff keeps switching the key:

In that first phrase alone he's gone through three different keys: D, B, and G-major. And then, in the last bar, he makes a musical *pun*. You know what a pun is: it's playing with a word—making it have two meanings at once, or giving it one meaning when you expect the other. It's like saying to your friend, "Give me a ring sometime, won't you?" and so he takes off his ring and gives it to you. That's just what Prokofieff does in the last phrase of the tune.

You see he leads you to expect this:

But instead, he slips one over on you with this:

You see how neatly he made the pun?

After you have listened to this beautiful, elegant joke, you will see how the word "incongruous" comes up again. That old-fashioned gavotte and those peculiar, punny harmonies just don't go together; and when you put them side by side they make a comical pair, like Mutt and Jeff. That's pure satire and also it's a beautiful piece. That's what makes it satire instead of parody; it's beautiful. Just as one of the great satires in literature is *Gulliver's Travels*, which is also a beautiful book. I don't expect you to fall down and cry with laughter when you hear it, but I do hope you get at least some of the fun out of it that I got when I was fifteen.

But maybe the most incongruous piece of music ever written is by Gustav Mahler, who actually made a whole movement of his *First Symphony* out of "*Frère Jacques*," the old round which I am sure you know.

Frè - re Jac - ques, Frè - re Jac - ques, dor - mez vous? dor - mez vous?

What he did was to put it into the minor, which makes that happy little tune suddenly very gloomy and sad, like this:

141

Then Mahler made it even sadder and gloomier (and therefore more *incongruous*) by putting it into a funeral march tempo, and giving it first to a solo double bass, which is a very gloomy instrument, and then to all the other gloomiest instruments he could think of.

It does seem strange to say that a funeral march is funny, but it *is* funny, because we know it's really our jolly friend "*Frère Jacques*," hiding there in that black gloomy disguise.

But now we're beginning to slip from satire into parody—into making musical fun just for the fun of it. That is what caricatures do, like cartoons of me with hair falling all over my face. That is why Gilbert and Sullivan's operettas are so funny; they *caricature* the style of serious opera; and because their operas are *not* serious, and all their characters are just silly cartoon people, the serious operatic style of the music seems *incongruous* and therefore funny.

Well, we started out our discussion of musical humor on a very high plane—Haydn, Prokofieff and Mahler, all the highest type of satire. Now let's take a plunge into the lower forms of musical humor—like parody and caricature—and even lower, into burlesque, which is just plain clowning. This is the kind of humor that some of us like the best: the real low-down kind, like a man slipping on a banana peel. That's still the funniest gag in show business. Why should it be? Why should we laugh when someone falls down?

Here we come to the central point of all humor: that all jokes *have* to be at the expense of someone or something; something has to be hurt or destroyed to make you laugh—a man's dignity, or an idea, or a word, or logic itself.

Something has to go, and it's usually *sense* that goes first—which is why, as we said before, we have *nonsense*. We go to the circus and see a clown catch on fire and douse himself with water. That's funny; we allow ourselves to laugh at the clown's expense because we know it's just a trick, and that the clown isn't really in danger.

Or we see a little automobile in the circus ring, and out comes a clown followed by another and then another and then three more and then twelve more, endlessly. How did they all get into that little car? It's impossible. We laugh louder and louder as more and more clowns keep issuing from the car; it's riotously funny, but again it's at the expense of something: of logic.

That's why we've laughed for years at Laurel and Hardy and Charlie Chaplin and the Marx Brothers. They make a hash of logic—they destroy sense, and we laugh our heads off, just as we do at the man slipping on the banana peel.

Now, how does this destroying element in humor apply to music? Well, you can destroy sense in music just as easily as in the circus ring or in the movies. Mozart did it many years ago in his famous "A Musical Joke," which ends up with all the instruments playing ghastly wrong notes. Ever since that Mozart joke, all kinds of composers have been doing the same thing. Wrong notes are the best way of getting a laugh in music; only they have to be written side by side with *right* notes, in order for them to sound wrong. As an example, just remember our experiment with the "Shave and a Haircut—Two Bits" tune. (See page 122.)

Again it's that business of being *incongruous*. And it takes a real sense of humor to do it well, and make it really funny. The modern Russian composer Shostakovich is a master of this kind of wrong-note joke. The

famous polka from his *Age of Gold* ballet is full of absurd tunes like this one:

He makes it even funnier by giving his cuckoo notes to very exaggerated instruments, way down in the tuba and way up in the piccolo and xylophone. It makes it sound even cuckoo-er.

The American composer Aaron Copland also makes us giggle through his way of destroying logic. In the "Burlesque," from his *Music for the Theatre*, he is busy destroying not so much the right *notes* as the right *rhythms*. Just when you expect the music to be equal—symmetrical, even—it loses it balance.

This music is constantly falling down and picking itself up again, and at the very end it slips for the last time, and just stays there, with a very puzzled look on its face.

Part of the humor in that piece by Copland is due to a lot of low, rude noises made by the low strings and the trombone, but mostly by the bassoon. The bassoon has always been called the clown of the orchestra. (I don't know why—it can sound pretty gloomy to me.)

Perhaps the most famous case of the bassoon's clowning is that well-known tune in *The Sorcerer's Apprentice* by Paul Dukas.

Ever since that sorcerer tune was written for the bassoon, movie composers have been calling on their bassoons to burp out the jokes every time they need comic effects. That's what has produced a new "art" called *Mickey-Mousing*, which makes the music follow the action *exactly*, step by step. Everyone has heard it: whenever Pluto crashes into a tree or Donald Duck is shot out of a cannon.

And it's not only in Mickey Mouse movies that you

hear Mickey Mouse music: it's in grown-up movies as well. Take a man trying to sneak home late at night holding his shoes in his hands, and, dollars to doughnuts, you'll be hearing that bassoon again.

It *is* an art—an art of imitating, as in that Rameau piece about the hen. But it's not very high art.

Well, now that we've sunk about as low as we can in musical humor, let's pull ourselves up again, and finish by talking about great *symphonic* humor.

This kind of humor is not supposed to be funny. All humor doesn't necessarily have to be funny. There's such a thing as just plain good humor, which means simply being in a good mood.

For "humor" is a strange word. Originally the word meant a fluid, a watery substance—that's where you get the word *humid*, meaning damp. In the old days doctors used to think that people had four of these humors, or fluids, in their bodies, which made them feel and act in different ways: there was blood, which made you energetic; and phlegm, which made you lazy and tired; there was choler, which made you angry; and melancholy, which made you—you guessed it—melancholy, sad. Then gradually the word "humor" came to mean not just fluids, but the states they put you in: energetic, tired, angry or sad. So you see, there are good humors and bad humors.

That's why you can say, "I'm in a bad humor today," meaning you're in a bad mood. Or, "I'm in a good humor today."

So symphonic humor does not have to be funny, but rather high-spirited, or playful, or devilish. Usually this kind of humor is to be found in the *scherzo* movement of a symphony. This Italian word *scherzo* means a joke; but in music it has come to mean any piece that is playful,

147

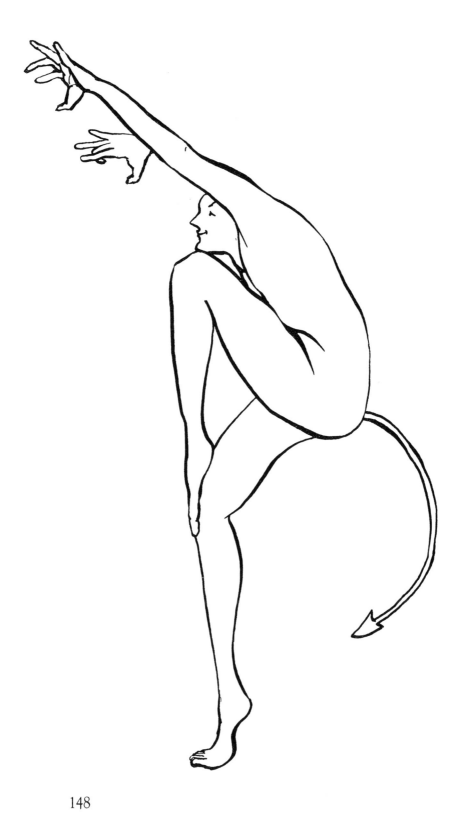

148

or lighthearted, or humorous in any way. Almost every symphony written contains some kind of scherzo—usually the third movement of the symphony. In the symphonies of Mozart and Haydn, the third movement was usually a minuet—graceful and elegant, and in moderate three-four time, like a waltz. But then came Beethoven, who took that minuet idea and speeded it up until it was going like a waltz on a hot-rod phonograph. In that way, the minuet became a scherzo. You can hear a marvelous example of a Beethoven scherzo in any one of his nine symphonies.

Taking their cue from Beethoven, composers have since made all kinds of changes in the third-movement scherzo idea, sometimes slowing it up again, sometimes making it the second movement, or sometimes even putting it into *two*-four time, or six-eight time, or anything they wanted. The scherzo from Brahms's *Fourth Symphony*, for instance, is in two-four time, and doesn't sound like any scherzo ever written before. The only things that make it a scherzo are that it *is* the third movement, it is playful, full of energy, short—as all jokes should be— and full of good humor.

This only goes to prove that there are all kinds of humor in the world, as well as music; and that all humor doesn't have to be a joke, or make you laugh. It can be strong and important, like *Gulliver's Travels*, and it can make you have deep emotions. But it's still *humor*, because it makes you feel *good* inside. And, after all, that's what music is for.

CHAPTER SEVEN

*W*hat Is a Concerto?

If some of you are alarmed at the small size of the orchestra on the stage today, don't worry. The Philharmonic has not come down with an epidemic of mumps or anything. You'll be seeing the rest of them soon enough, and in a few minutes I think you'll understand why we are beginning this program with such a tiny orchestra.

This one is our last program of the season, and whenever people come to the end of anything, they always start asking themselves big questions like "What are we really here for? What are we trying to accomplish? Are we really accomplishing it?"—questions like that. I guess everyone does the same. When the end of a year rolls around, people always begin asking themselves basic questions, trying to take stock of their lives, of what they've done all year, wondering how to change, and what resolutions to make for the New Year.

My big question is: have we been helping you to come closer to good music? Are you beginning to understand a little more about it, and learning not to be scared of it? Most of my young friends that I talk to say yes; that they *are* feeling closer to music—sort of friendly to it. They have begun to feel that music isn't such a hard, strange business, too grown-up or complicated or sissy-ish or whatever. But one thing they all worry about—and that's the words about music: hard words like *recapitulation, fugue, rondo, andantino, sinfonietta,* G# *minor, the inversion of the second theme backwards at the augmented fifth,* and double-talk like that.

Well, I've tried not to use those words, whenever I could do without them; and when I've *had* to say them, I have tried to explain them as clearly as I could. But there are some musical words which can't be explained in a second; it takes time to learn about them; and what's more, it takes listening to the actual music they describe before you really know what they mean. One of those hard words that bothers people is the Italian word *concerto* (pronounced: *con-chair-toe*), which you really should know about. It's a simple Italian word, which means a "concert"—practically the same word. But in music the word has come to mean a lot of other things, as we will find out.

The original meaning of "concert" is the idea of things happening together: a football team performs in concert; the players make a *concerted* effort to win. As a certain magazine would say,[1] it means "togetherness," which is a lovely idea, but rather an ugly word. Well, in music the word "concert" means the "togetherness" of musicians, who come together to play or sing in a group.

Ever since music began to be written for audiences like yourselves, composers have use the word *concerto* to name their pieces. All kinds of different musical forms used to be called concertos, even though they weren't pieces we

would call concertos today. You see, names can be used very loosely. All sorts of different pieces used to be called symphonies, too, or sonatas. Those were also just general words to describe the same pieces the word *concerto* described: *symphony* also meant musical sounds being made together; and *sonata* meant simply anything that sounded, nothing more.

But slowly, as years passed, the names began to be used more strictly. *Sonata* began to mean a piece for any solo instrument, like a harpsichord, or for a violin, or a flute, or a lute, or a cello, with or without a harpsichord to accompany it. Now our job of word-hunting becomes easier. Do you know what a trio is? Simply a sonata for three instruments; then there's *quartet*, a sonata for four instruments, any four instruments. Now answer the next two yourselves: A quintet is a sonata for how many instruments? And an octet is a sonata for how many?

Right, if you guessed five and eight. Moving forward— this is important—a sonata for a whole orchestra is called a *symphony*. Isn't that simple? And a symphony that features a soloist, or a little group of soloists, separate from the big orchestra group, is called a *concerto*. And there you have it. That wasn't so hard, was it?

Now that we know that much, we can find out the rest by looking at and listening to different kinds of concertos. We're going to go way back to those early baroque days of Bach and Handel, when the word "concerto" was still used pretty loosely, and could mean almost anything. But there was a thing back then called a *concerto grosso*, which in Italian means a *big* concerto. This simply meant a piece, usually in three movements, that was written for a big orchestra with a little orchestra attached to it— just like the earth which travels around through space with its little moon traveling along next to it.

The idea of togetherness is there, all right; and it's fine for all these people of the big orchestra to be playing together. But if you think about it for a second, you realize that they can't be playing together all the time. That would become boring because there wouldn't be any relief from a sound that was always the same. So that's why composers invented the idea of the small group, called the *concertino*, alongside the big group; and they simply took turns playing with the themes—first the big group, then the small one, then only part of the small one, then the big group again, then both groups together.

That makes *variety*, change, contrast, which keeps you interested. Besides, it gives the musicians in the small group a chance to show off a little by themselves. An example of this kind of concerto is by the great Italian composer Vivaldi, who wrote hundreds of concertos for many different kinds of instruments.[2]

Vivaldi was one of those marvelous composers who never seemed to run out of ideas—and he never seemed to run out of instruments to write them for. He spent about thirty years of his life as director of music in a girls' school,[3] where he had a fine all-female choir, and a strange all-female orchestra made up of whatever instruments the girls happened to be able to play. Of course, this made him write concertos with some very peculiar little groups in them. One of my favorites is for an orchestra that actually features in its concertino two mandolins.[4]

That's pretty unusual. Some of the other instruments Vivaldi wrote for in this piece don't exist any more—like the *tiorbi* (or "theorboe"), which was a sort of big guitar; so we perform the tiorba parts on harps. Then there were two instruments called *tromba marina* (that is, "trumpet-marines"), which were, strange to say, stringed instruments—great big things with only one string, and which gave out a sound, a very loud sound rather like a bad trumpet played out of tune. So we play those parts on real trumpets—played, we hope, in tune. Besides we have a bass oboe, replacing the old *salmo*,[5] which is long since dead and gone, and finally we have two flutes (regular flutes), and that's all. Those twelve instruments make up the concertino. The main orchestra consists of the harpsichord and the usual strings, with the solo violin and the solo cello featured in the concertino group.

All together, it's quite a hodgepodge of peculiar instruments; but they still make a very small orchestra compared to present-day standards. A big concert hall stage certainly does look bare with them; but what a delicious sound these twenty-three instruments can make! It's lovely music—you should check it out.

Around the time that Vivaldi was writing his concertos in Italy, the great composer Bach was writing *his* concertos in Germany. Perhaps the most famous are the series of six called the *Brandenburg Concertos*, and we're going to look at the final movement of one of the best known, *Number Five*. The orchestra gets bigger; the stage begins to fill up. But the remarkable thing about it is that as the orchestra gets bigger, the little concertino group, or soloist group, gets smaller. In Bach's *Fifth Brandenburg Concerto* there are only three soloists: violin—there always seems to be a solo violin—a solo flute and the harpsichord.

In the last movement you can clearly hear that contrast idea I just mentioned, as the theme gets tossed around from the violin to the flute to the harpsichord, and then to the whole orchestra, and then—well, see it for yourselves.

History moves on. We now reach the classical age of Mozart and Haydn. The orchestra gets even bigger; and as the orchestra expands the concertino group dwindles. Why was this happening? It's because the show-off element of concertos was getting more important all the time.

As time went on, the number of solo players in the concertino group grew smaller and smaller; but their importance as soloists grew larger and larger. So now we arrive at the magnificent concerto by Mozart for only two solo instruments, a violin and a viola. (As we saw before, no composer seems to be able to do without the violin.) These soloists really get to show their stuff. The orchestra gets to play too, of course; but most of the time they are just playing accompaniment to the two big shots who are the real stars of the piece. In this instance, it's called a *Sinfonia Concertante*, or a concerted symphony— you get the meaning?

But the soloists' greatest moment comes toward the end of the second movement, when the big orchestra stops completely, to let the two big shots have a field day of showing off in what is called a *cadenza*. Remember *that* hard word: cadenza, which comes between a big pause and the last *cadence* of a piece (cadenza-cadence, you see?) and where the soloist or soloists can really go to town. The great thing about this beautiful slow movement is that it's so inspired that even Mozart's cadenza is beautiful—not just a show-off cadenza, but great and deeply moving music.

So far we've looked at concertos for various kinds of groups, of different sizes, from the Vivaldi,[6] which had a nine-instrument concertino, right up to this last Mozart duet. Where is it all leading? Obviously, down to the single solo performer: one pianist, one violinist, one kazoo player, whatever it is; but one, that's the main thing: the star, the virtuoso, the Jascha Heifetz, the Van Cliburn, the Pablo Casals.[7] By Mozart's time the solo concerto was already pretty well developed, especially for the piano (he wrote twenty-seven piano concertos alone!). Then Beethoven came along and wrote five great piano concertos, Brahms wrote two, and many composers have been doing it ever since. To say nothing of all the great violin and cello concertos. The solo concerto had come to stay. Almost every orchestra concert anywhere in the world probably has a solo concerto on its program.

But there's a danger in the rise of the solo concerto; and that danger is the leaning too hard on the show-off side of things. There are so many concertos that are useful and interesting more for their virtuoso display, their flashy technical goods, than for their real musical worth. In certain violin concertos I could name (but won't), the whole point is in the cadenza, where the orchestra stops and lets the violinist go on endlessly showing off how marvelous he is, like an Olympic pole-vault champion. Such concertos are usually praised for being "violinistic," that is, written to show the instrument in its most dazzling light; and there are terrible piano concertos described as "pianistic," and lots of bad cello concertos that are "cellistic," another ugly word. But a great composer, a Mozart, Beethoven, Brahms, Schumann, Tchaikovsky, Ravel, Stravinsky or Bartók—they save the day because they could write concertos that show off the soloist beautifully and can also be great music at the same time.

An example of a great violin concerto is the Mendelssohn *Violin Concerto*. Here at last stands the virtuoso star in all his solitary splendor, in music that makes a perfect combination of the "violinistic" element, the flashy-display element, and of serious, great, music. The orchestra is by now practically full size, and they have much more interesting things to do than simply accompanying the big shot; but then the soloist has such difficult, fancy things to do that it evens out the balance. Here's a "flashy bit" from the concerto's last movement:

In our own time, in the twentieth century, composers have shown a strong tendency to go back to the old concerto grosso idea. It's not that they don't write solo concertos any more; they do by the dozens. It's just that the solo concerto has become so big and so showy that certain composers have begun to feel a need for the simple old forms of classical days. Such composers are called neoclassical composers, and so we've begun to have a new form in music: the concerto for orchestra, which, as we've seen, is really a very old form dug up again. But these concertos are for modern orchestras, huge as compared to the old ones of Bach and Vivaldi. So these modern concertos have a great many things to show off. We have concertos for orchestra by Bloch, Piston, Stravinsky, Hindemith and many others; but perhaps the most showy and effective and beautiful of all is by the great Hungarian composer Béla Bartók.

His *Concerto for Orchestra* shows off (or I should say, lights up) every little department of this splendid body of musicians, so that everyone in the orchestra gets a chance to shine. Imagine, that in the tiny fourth movement of this concerto, which lasts only four minutes, you can hear all these solos: first an oboe playing the tune, then a flute, a clarinet, a horn—all playing that same tune.

After this comes a new romantic tune for the violas, which is repeated for the violins. Then another jolly tune on the clarinet, with solo trombones sliding away deep down like caged animals at the circus, followed by another growling tuba solo; then a whole cadenza for the

161

flute alone; and finally the piccolo has its little say. All that in four minutes, and it's practically everybody. In the fifth movement, which is the final one of the concerto, everyone gets a workout, especially the strings, who really have to work for a living at an unbelievable rate of speed. But then everybody eventually gets into the act. This is modern music at its very best, a delightful and thrilling piece—and the most democratic concerto ever written—a concerto for a hundred soloists.

Folk Music in the Concert Hall

Folk songs and folk dances are really the heart of music, the very beginning of all music. You'd be amazed at how much of the big, complicated concert music we hear grows right out of them.

For instance, here's a pretty tune that might be a folk song.

Somehow it has that folk-song flavor, like something a lot of people might sing together in a bus, or on a hike, or around the campfire. But it's not sung in any of those places. It's not even sung at all. It's written for a clarinet, and it comes from a symphony by Mozart.

Maybe that surprises you—because it seems so simple and natural, not like the kind of complicated and grand music we usually think of as being in a symphony. But that's just what I mean: almost all symphonic music has folk music in it, in one way or another.

What *is* folk music, anyway? Folk music expresses the nature of a particular people or nation or race. You can almost always tell something about them by simply listening to their folk songs. Most people like to think that this kind of music just grew, like Topsy, naturally, without any composer. That's a wrong idea, because a folk song or folk dance was always written by *somebody*, only we don't usually know who it was. Somebody *did* write it; at least, he made it up, and it was passed on from fathers to sons and mothers to daughters for hundreds of years, without necessarily being written down.

Most of the folk songs we know belong to the past, when the different peoples of the earth were more separate from one another, and their characters and different natures were easier to tell apart. Sometimes these songs reflect the *climate* of a certain country; or they tell us something about its geography; or even tell us something about what the people do, like being shepherds, or cowboys, or miners, or whatever.

But most important of all, folk songs reflect the rhythms and accents and speeds of the way a particular people *talk*. In other words, their language—especially the language of their poetry—grows into musical notes. And these speaking-rhythms and accents finally pass from folk music into the art music, or opera, or concert music of a people; and that is what makes Tchaikovsky sound

Russian, and Verdi sound Italian, and Gershwin sound American.

It all comes from the folk music, which in turn comes first of all from the way we speak. And that's the important thing we have to learn. First of all, take a Hungarian folk song that begins like this:

Why do we know immediately that that's a Hungarian tune? (I mean, *besides* the fact that it's got Hungarian words.) It's because the Hungarian language has a strange thing about it: almost all the words in it are accented on the first sylable. JÖjjön HAza Edes Anyam. That's how you can almost always tell a Hungarian speaking English. He'll say, "I don't UNderstand, BEcause I am HUNgarian." And that same accent naturally pops up in the music:

—all the stresses BElong at the BEginning.

And so it's just as natural, when a great Hungarian composer like Béla Bartók writes his music, that he should compose in that same accent. Just look at this phrase from Bartók's beautiful *Music for Strings, Percussion and Celesta*:

Do you see how that tune is like a string of words in a sentence, each one with a big accent (>) at the BEginning? And that's not even folk music any more; it's already moved into the concert hall.

The same thing is true of all music. It grows out of a people's folk music, which grows out of their language. Look at French, for instance. French is a language that has almost no strong accents at all. Almost every syllable is equal—not in length, but in accent. A Frenchman might introduce me like this, "*Permettez-moi de vous présenter Monsieur Bernstein*," with every syllable getting the same, even stress. But the minute you hear someone saying, "*PerMETtez-MOI de vous PREsenTER MonSIEUR BERNstein*," then you know he's not a Frenchman.

And these equal stresses show up just as clearly in French folk music. Do you know this charming French folk song?

na - vi - gué, o - hé - o - hé! [2]

Do you see how equal all the syllables are? There are no "accents" (>'s); only the natural ones caused by certain syllables' being *held longer* than others. But you don't *hit* any note harder than any other, as you do in the Hungarian tune we just saw. It's all smooth and even.

And that's exactly the smoothness and evenness we hear in French concert music, like this phrase from one of Satie's *Gymnopédies* for piano:

So it goes through all the languages. Italian, for instance, is famous for its long beautiful vowels, as, for example, in the familiar song "Santa Lucia":

San - ta— Lu - ci - a, San - ta Lu - ci - a,

And this lingering on the vowels is reflected in much Italian instrumental music, as in this long, singing melody line from Vivaldi's *Concerto for Strings* (F. XI, No. 2):

169

Spanish, on the other hand, doesn't linger so much on the vowels; the consonants are more important. Like this song, "La Bamba," which says that "to dance the Bamba you need a bit of grace, and a bit of something else"— and so the folk music comes out crisp and rhythmic, like the language:

And so it is with Spanish concert music. Have you ever heard these sharp, exicting Spanish rhythms in Manuel De Falla's ballet, *The Three-Cornered Hat?*

German, of course, is a very heavy language, with long words, and very long combinations of sounds: "*Soll ich schlürfen, untertauchen, süss in Düften mich verhauchen?*"

170

is one of the *simpler* lines from Wagner's opera *Tristan und Isolde*. And so German symphonic music tends to be heavier and longer and more—well, *important*—than, say, French or Spanish music:

And as for English—that depends on what English you're talking about. *English* English is one thing; and the folk songs from England are unmistakable—tripping and light, and quick with the tongue, just as the British speak:

But now what kind of English is this?

Of course, it's Western cowboy English. And you see how different the music is too—how lazy and drawling. And just as different is the English of New York City,

171

with it slapdash syncopations, and its tough charm:

Jazzily

"FUGUE FOR TINHORNS" From
GUYS AND DOLLS by Frank Loesser

I got the horse right here _ the name is

Paul Re - vere _

And that accent is heard in the concert hall in all kinds
of American instrumental pieces, such as Gershwin's
Piano Concerto:

Lazily   from Movement II

pp stacc.   *etc.*

All this still doesn't explain that Mozart melody we
started out with. But that's not too hard. It's the middle
part of the Minuet, the third movement, of Mozart's
Symphony in E-flat; and the thing that makes the tune so
enchanting is *not* that it's a folk tune, but that it's *like* a
folk tune. We could even put words to it and *call* it a
folk tune:

I was go-ing to Straw-ber-ry_ Fair

173

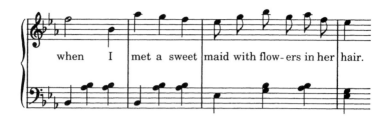

when I met a sweet maid with flow-ers in her hair.

Only this time the tune is from Austria, so the English words don't seem quite right. The melody has all the creamy sweetness of *Austrian* speech, and, what's more, it has some of those Tyrolean *hup-tsa-tsas*—in the accompaniment—that make *that* folk music so famous:

Hup - tsa - tsa, Hup - tsa - tsa, Hup - tsa - tsa, Hup - tsa tsa,

The Minuet is *concert* music by Mozart, but it could never have been written if the simple Austrian folk music hadn't come first.

Of course there is a great deal of concert music that does make use of *actual* folk material. Only think of *The Moldau* by the Czech composer Smetana, the *Fourth Symphony* of Tschaikovsky, the *Indian Symphony (Sinfonía India)* by the Mexican composer Carlos Chavez, or the *Symphony No. 2* by the American Charles Ives.

This last one is a perfect example to concentrate on, because not only does Ives quote from real folk tunes, but he also imitates the spirit of American folk music in general, just as Mozart did in his minuet.

Charles Ives was a salty old Yankee who lived, up to his death a few years ago, in Danbury, Connecticut. The really surprising thing about Ives was that he made his living not by music at all, but by selling insurance. But music was what he loved most in the world. And even though he could compose only at night and on weekends, he was a first-class composer—perhaps the first great composer in American history.

He was also one of the first American composers to use folk songs and folk dances in his concert music. It was his way of being American—to take marching tunes and hymns and patriotic songs and popular country music and develop them all together into big symphonic works. In the last movement of his *Second Symphony* you will find yourself listening to tunes that *sound* like barn dance music, tunes that *sound* like Stephen Foster melodies, tunes that *sound* like fife and drum music; but more than this, you will also hear *real* barn dance tunes like "Turkey in the Straw":

With pep

—and *real* folk songs such as "Long, Long Ago":

Lightly and slowly

and a *real* Stephen Foster tune—"Camptown Races":

Jauntily

and a *real* bugle call—"Reveille":

and to top it all off, a *real* quotation from that grand old American tune—"Columbia the Gem of the Ocean":

March tempo

176

It all adds up to a rousing jamboree, like a Fourth of July celebration, finished off at the very end by a wild yelp of laughter made by the orchestra playing a chord of all the notes in the rainbow at once[3]:

—as if to say, "WOW!"

Listening to this work is like hearing American folk music dressed up in white tie and tails for a symphony concert!

*W*hat Is Impressionism?

In this chapter we're going to give most of our attention to one piece of music, a piece about the sea, by the great French composer Debussy. You may have heard him called *Day*-bussy or even De-*byou*-sy; but however you pronounce his name, Claude De-bus-sy wrote a masterpiece called *La Mer* (which means "The Sea"), and it is probably the most famous piece of music ever written about the sea.

When I was a youngster in Boston, I could hardly imagine that there were people who might never have seen the ocean in their lives—people in Winnipeg, for instance, smack in the middle of Canada. Now, if I wanted to tell someone in Winnipeg what the sea is like, I could do it fairly easily by facts or figures, or by sending him a picture postcard from Coney Island. But that wouldn't give him the real *quality* of the sea, what it feels like to look at it, smell it, hear it, in all its variety of stillness and storminess and playfulness. What our friend in Winnipeg would need is an *impression* of the sea, not just facts and figures. And that brings us to the subject at hand—*impressionism*.

This sea piece by Debussy is what is called an *impressionistic* piece of music: that is, it tells you no facts at all; it is not a realistic description, but instead it is all color and movement and *suggestion*.

That was the idea that all impressionist artists had in mind, whether they were poets, or painters, or composers—and, by the way, they're almost all French; and it was a French idea that in art you can make a deeper effect by suggestion than you can by realistic description.

The Cathedral at Rouen, PAINTING BY CLAUDE MONET. BY COURTESY OF THE MUSEUM OF FINE ARTS, BOSTON.

Now, of course, the real job of music is *not* to describe anything at all, but just to be music, and to give us excitement and pleasure and inspiration only through the notes. (I hope you remember that from the first chapter in this book.) But some music has occasionally been written *about* things, about nature or stories or ideas, and such music is called program music. Impressionistic music is almost *always* program music; that is, it's *about* something—scenery or a poem or a picture. The whole idea of impressionism began with painters—French painters like Manet, Monet, Renoir and all the other famous names.

The Cathedral at Rouen. BY COURTESY OF THE FRENCH GOVERNMENT TOURIST OFFICE

181

Have you ever looked at an impressionistic French painting? I'm sure you have, but maybe you didn't know it; you just saw a picture that seemed to you blurry or hazy, that didn't have a "real" sort of look. On page 180, we have an example: a painting, by the great impressionist Monet, of the front of the cathedral at Rouen. You see how misty it is? You can almost not tell *what* it is at first sight. Now, just for fun, take a look at the ordinary photograph of that same cathedral, on page 181. See the difference?

Now you see the hard, clean outlines and edges and shapes. A realistic painter would want to make the cathedral as real as possible, with the light and shapes exact, like the photograph. But not Monet, the impressionist painter; he wants you to see not so much a cathedral as light itself, and colors, as they look to him reflecting *on* a cathedral. This is almost like a *dream* of a cathedral, an impression of it, a suggestion, as we said before, as seen at a certain moment of the day when the light was a certain way. Monet painted about thirty different pictures of this same view in different lights—bright morning, cloudy afternoon and others; and this one is the cathedral painted in the sunset, which has turned the stone into a dazzling, blurry dance of blues and oranges and mauves. That is one *impression* of this cathedral at Rouen. (I am sorry we cannot reproduce the exact coloring in this book, but even a photograph of the painting gives the general effect of the blurriness.)

Of course, music is completely different from painting in that it can't *ever* really be realistic. Notes can't ever give you the exact measurements of a cathedral, or the exact shape of somebody's nose. But music can be more or less realistic in its own way: that is, it can have sharp, clear outlines like these harmonies:

182

Do you feel the hazy, indefinite quality of that last group of chords? Well, those are impressionistic chords.

Or music can have a straightforward, clear theme, like this theme of Beethoven's, which you know:

That's clear, direct—like your father saying, "Go to bed!"

Turn off that light!

183

Or music can *suggest* with fuzzy little wisps of melody as Debussy does:

—which is like hinting at pleasant dreams. Suggestion, you see? That's impressionism.

But now let's get down to the most interesting part, and find out just what these strange, new sounds of impressionism are. I say *new* sounds, even though they're fifty years old or so,[1] and they've become so imitated in American popular songs and in Hollywood scores and record-album arrangements and what not that they seem like the most normal, everyday sounds to us. And yet, compared to the sounds of Bach, Beethoven and Brahms, they're absolutely brand-new, and in the hands of a master like Debussy they sound as fresh today as they ever did.

Well, what are some of the ways Debussy invented for getting these sounds?

This comes from a piano piece of his called *Voiles*, or "Sails," which paints a dreamy impression of graceful gliding sailboats in the afternoon sun off in the hazy distance. How does he get that hazy sound? The method he uses is one of the most important in impressionistic music. It's called using whole tones. Do you know what a whole tone is? It's simple: two half tones. Now, if you remember that the step from any note on the piano to the note just next to it, whether it's black or white, is a step of a half tone, you can see that the entire piano keyboard is made up of only half tones, one after another.

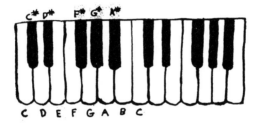

The · shows whole tone scale.

Out of these half tones, we make what we call our chromatic scale:

We can also make all the other scales (see Chapter Fourteen on modes), like our ordinary major scale, which is some whole tones and some half tones:

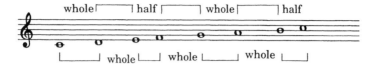

But if we start at the same place and go up only by *whole* tones, then we get Debussy's scale:

—which, as you can hear when you play it, is much less definite and final-sounding than the ordinary scales. And so out of this scale he has made this delicious little impression of hazy sailboats in the half-light, floating, airy, without any definite outlines.

However, that's not exactly what you'd call a great melody—a tune you go out whistling. Debussy didn't often write long, continuous melodies, as Schubert or Tchaikovsky did; that isn't what interested him so much as *bits* of melody that could make an atmosphere. But now here's an exception: this little piece has a real tune:

What impression does this tune give you? What does it suggest to you? Actually, it's about a girl with flaxen hair, and I suppose, because the music is so simple and child-like and pure, that she's probably very young, and maybe a country girl, a shepherdess or something. But the *mu-*

sical thing that makes this tune so charming is the use of another special kind of scale, this time called the *pentatonic* scale. All that means is that it is a scale having five notes—penta-tonic:

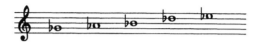

You can find this short little scale easily on your piano by playing only the black keys.

This is an old scale that has been used for centuries in folk music all over the world. I'm sure you've all heard Chinese music made out of this scale, as well as Scottish bagpipe music, African music, or American Indian music:

And so, how logical it is to use this black-note scale for simple, folklike country music as Debussy did in his piece about the little blond girl. (Of course, there's one *white* note that sneaked in there—but we'll forgive Debussy for that.)

You see, he was always searching for new colors, new sounds, and so he used every unusual kind of scale, old or new, that he could lay his hands on. He even went back to the ancient Greek scales, or modes, as they are called; and also to the old modes that were used in church music over a thousand years ago. For example, the mixolydian mode:

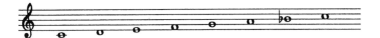

Here is that mode used in Debussy's famous piano piece *The Sunken Cathedral*:

But it's not only strange scales that make Debussy's music sound different; he also used the same scales as everyone else—major or minor—but used them in new ways, by making chords out of them that no one had ever heard before. For instance, he would take this ordinary chord of three notes:

and then he would add to it:

then add more:

189

and MORE:

and MORE:

until it became a new, complicated, misty, impression-istic chord. Or he would alter notes of that chord slightly to give a sort of special color to it:

Can you hear the special "color" of that chord?

This is the same sort of harmony that you can find in dozens of pieces by Debussy, with titles like "Goldfish," "Moonlight" (*"Clair de Lune"*), "Reflections in the Water," "Clouds," and "Footsteps in the Snow." All these pieces reflect light in some way—like the shim-mering light of the water in the goldfish bowl—all painted by these richly colored harmonies, just like those special colors we talked about in Monet's cathedral paint-ing.

I'm not going to try to explain just what these chords are made of; that would be too complicated. But I would like to explain to you one very special way Debussy gets these rich blurry colors in his harmonies. It's called *bi-tonality*, and it means two different harmonies at once—that is, music written in two different keys at the same

190

time! It's as though I started the "Vienna Woods" waltz in one key:

and came in with the tune in another key:

Pretty peculiar, isn't it? But that's bitonality; and when Debussy uses it, it comes out not peculiar at all, but rich, blurry and impressionistic, as in this marvelous piece of his in which the accompaniment is in one key:

and the tune in another:

But together, the two keys make a strange, beautiful impressionistic sound—dark and passionate:

By the way, this piece, as you've probably guessed from the tango accompaniment, is a Spanish sort of music called *La Puerta del Vino,* and the fact that it's Spanish in its style tells us still another thing about impressionism. Debussy was always looking for new sounds—he was attracted to music of exotic places, like Spain, or the Orient, or ancient Greece, or even to jazz from America. Don't forget that Debussy was composing at a time when jazz—or ragtime, as it was then called—was just beginning to sweep the world. So he borrowed some of our jazzy rhythms and ideas, and wrote a few pieces like this one, which I'm sure you've heard, called "The Golliwog's Cakewalk":

192

That will show you that Debussy didn't always write slow, serious music, as you may have begun to think. He had a wonderful sense of humor, too.

Now, I think, we're ready to have a go at that great sea piece of Debussy's, *La Mer*, which I mentioned at the beginning of this chapter. You're an expert now on impressionism, and ready to enjoy one of the greatest works ever written for orchestra. I wish we could provide you with a record of *La Mer*, but at least I can *tell* you a little bit about the music which may encourage you to buy a recording. The first movement is called "From Dawn to Noon on the Sea," and in it you get all kinds of impressions or suggestions: the absolute stillness of the ocean just before dawn, which comes right at the beginning; then the first spooky rays of light coming up; the first faint cries of sea birds; the waters beginning to stir and rock as the first breeze comes up. Then, as the movement goes on, there is a bright new sound from the cellos and horns, which is like the sudden appearance of the sun over the horizon:

How golden that is! From there on, the music grows in power and color and movement, until at the very end the sun has climbed to the height of noon and hangs there, blazing in space. This is a great moment of musical painting that Debussy has made with his last chord, by suddenly taking away all the high notes and all the low notes, and leaving only the brass chord hanging there in the middle like a ball of fire in space:

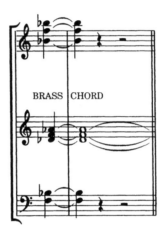

You can practically see the sun shining there like a big ball, blazing at noontime. It is a marvelous piece of tone-painting—for that's just what it is: painting for the ear instead of the eye.

Now we arrive at the second movement, called "The Play of the Waves," which is a light, sparkling impression of the sea in its most playful mood. In it you'll hear all the scales and harmonies and tricks we've been talking about: a wavy wisp of a tune in an old church mode (the Lydian mode):

194

Then you'll hear real splashes of foam coming up out of the waves, all made of the whole-tone scale:

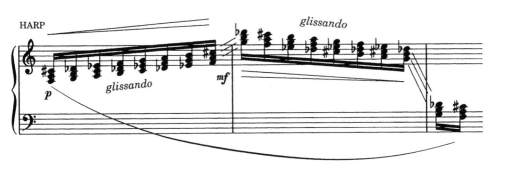

What a wonderful way to paint waves! And then those rich, blurry harmonies:

There are even Spanish rhythms in this movement, like this bolero rhythm that suddenly comes in the middle:

195

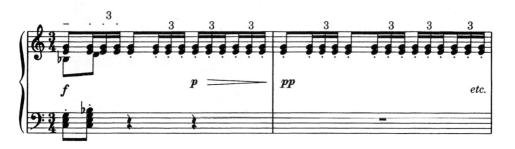

And you'll hear bitonality and all the rest. No jazz, though.

If you can manage to hear a recording of all three movements of *La Mer*, or hear it at a concert or on the radio, you can find many beautiful examples of all these devices we've been talking about. But at least this second movement will give you a delicious sample. And I hope that it makes you love this music as much as I do.

It's almost impossible to end this discussion of impressionism without a mention of the other great French impressionist composer, Maurice Ravel. It's funny how many great men of music seem to come in pairs: Bach—Handel, Mozart—Haydn, Bruckner—Mahler, and Debussy—Ravel. These last two giants wrote most of the outstanding works of impressionism that exist in the world. Ravel's music is very much like Debussy's only it has a special personality of its own, too. But that's a whole other discussion, as you will read at the end of the next chapter.

*W*hat Is a Melody?

Most people, when they think of music, think of melody right away. To some people it's almost the same thing—melody equals music. And they are right, in a way, because what *is* music, anyway, but sounds that change and move along in time? And what is practically a definition of melody too: a series of notes that move along in time, one after the other. Well, if that's true, then it is almost impossible to write music that does *not* have melody in it. I mean, if a melody is simply one note coming after another, how can a composer *avoid* writing melodies even if he just writes separate notes? He *must* be writing melodies all the time. Look. He writes one note:

—then he writes another:

—and he's already got a tiny two-note melody.

That's a melody—*sort* of. If he adds a third note:

—it begins to sound a little more melodious, and if he then adds a few more:

—well, we've got Mendelssohn's "Wedding March":

Allegro Vivace

You see how simple it is? Where there's music, there's melody. You can't have one without the other. Then why do so many people complain about music that has *no* melody? Some people say they don't like Johann Sebastian Bach fugues, because they don't find them melodic. And others say the same thing about Richard Wagner operas, and others about modern music, and others about jazz. What do you suppose they mean when they say "it's not melodic"? What are they talking about? Isn't any string of notes a melody? Well, I think the answer lies in the fact that melody can be a lot of different things: it can be a tune, or it can be a theme, or a motive, or a long melodic line, or a bass line, or an inner voice— all those things; and the minute we understand the differences among all those kinds of melody, then I think we'll be able to understand the whole problem.

You see, people usually think of melody as a *tune*, something you can go out whistling, that's easy to remember, that "sticks in your mind." What's more, a tune almost never goes out of the range of the normal human singing voice—that is, too high or too low. Nor should a tune have phrases that last longer than a normal breath can sing them. After all, melody is the *singing* side of music, just as rhythm is the dancing side. But the most important thing about a tune is that it is usually complete in itself—that is, it seems to have a beginning, middle and end and leaves you feeling satisfied. In other words, it's a song, like Gershwin's "Summertime," or Schubert's "Serenade," or your favorite number by Simon and Garfunkel.

But in symphonic music, which is what we're mostly concerned with here, tunes aren't exactly in order, because being complete in themselves, tunes don't cry out for further development. And, development is the main thing in symphonic music (See Chapter Four, "What Makes Music Symphonic?")—the growing and changing of a melodic seed into a big symphonic tree. So that seed *mustn't* be a complete tune, but rather a melody that leaves something still to be said, to be developed—and that kind of melody is called a *theme*.

Well, that's already a problem for those people who are always expecting music to consist of full-blown tunes, and so they'll naturally find these incomplete themes less "melodic." I suppose, then, that they should complain about the famous four-note theme that opens Beethoven's *Fifth Symphony:*

—that's hardly melodic at all. Or they complain about this theme from his *Seventh Symphony:*

—which is mostly harping on the same note. But both of these themes *are* kinds of melodies, even though they're not *tunes*. That's the important thing to remember. They're not tunes, but they're themes. Of course, there *are* symphonic themes that are much more melodious than those. Only think of Tchaikovsky's *Sixth Symphony:*

Why that's practically a whole tune in itself.

Now what is it about that big, tuneful theme that makes it so attractive and beloved, besides the fact that Tchaikovsky was a melodic genius? The answer is *repetition*—either exact repetition or slightly altered repetition, *within the theme itself.* It's that repetition that makes the melody stick in your mind; and it's the melodies that stick in your mind that are likely to please you the most. Popular songwriters know this, and that's why they repeat their phrases so often. Just think of that ancient song hit, "Mack the Knife," repeating over and over:

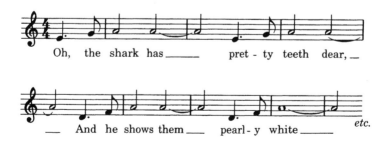

Well, the same technique works just as well in symphonic themes. For instance, let's just see how Tchaikovsky went about building up that lovely theme of his by simply repeating his ideas in a certain arranged order—what I like to call the 1-2-3 method. In fact, so many famous themes are formed by exactly this method that I think you ought to know about it. Here's how it works: first of all, there is a short idea, or phrase:

—second, the same phrase is repeated, but with a small variation:

—and third, the tune takes off in a flight of inspiration:

1, 2, & 3—like a 3-stage rocket, or like the countdown in a race: "On your mark, get set, go!" Or in target practice: "Ready, aim, fire!" Or in a movie studio: "Lights, camera, action!" It's always the same, 1, 2, and

3! There are so many examples of this melodic technique I almost don't know where to begin. But let's take, for example, our good old standby, Beethoven's *Fifth.* One, on your mark:

—two, get set:

—three, go!

Or, do you know that haunting theme in the César Franck Symphony? It's the same thing. First, there's a phrase:

—then he repeats it with a slight change, a rising intensity:

—then comes the gratifying fulfillment—the takeoff:

Or the same thing is true of Mozart's "*Haffner*" Symphony: It goes: Ready!—

—Aim!—

—Fire!

And so on. There are millions of them, examples of this 1-2-3 design; and don't forget that the heart of the matter is repetition: 2 is always a repeat of 1, and 3 is the takeoff.

Now that we know a few of the secrets that make music sound *melodic*, let's start looking for some of the reasons why people find certain kinds of music *un*melodic. We've already discovered that what appeals to people most as melody is a fully spun-out tune, and when instead they get an incomplete tune or a theme, they begin to have trouble. So you can imagine that when they hear music made out of melodies that are even shorter than themes, they have even more trouble. For example, that famous opening of Beethoven's *Fifth* again:

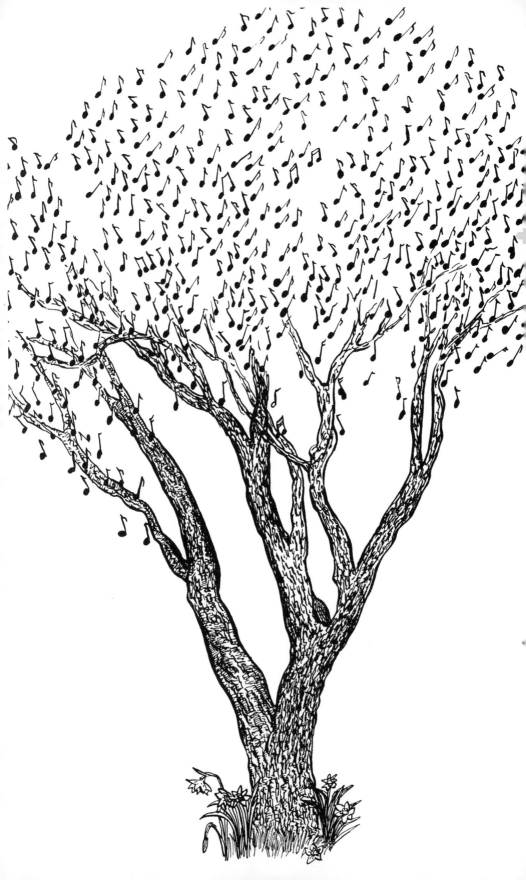

—is so short it's not really even a theme, but what is called a motive. Now a motive can be as little as two notes, or three or four—a bare melodic seed—the raw material out of which longer melodic lines are made.

You remember I said that certain people find Wagner's operas unmelodic? This is why: because Wagner usually constructed those huge operas of his out of tiny little motives, instead of writing regular tunes such as the Italian opera composers used. But how wrong they are to say that Wagner doesn't write *melody*! He writes nothing *but* melody, only it's melody that's made out of motives. Let me show you how. You've all heard the prelude to his great opera *Tristan and Isolde,* I'm sure. It begins with a four-note motive:

Immediately comes another motive, also of four notes:

The exciting thing is the way Wagner puts these two motives together. He makes the second motive begin smack on the end of the first one, so that the last note of one and the first note of the other are joined, locking the two motives securely together. Like this:

Now he adds some marvelous harmony underneath, and this is what you get: the beginning of *Tristan and Isolde*:

That's already much more than a motive, or even two motives. It has become what is called a *phrase*, just as a series of words in language is called a phrase. And Wagner, by using this method of joining motives together and making phrases out of them, and then sentences out of the phrases, and paragraphs out of the sentences, finally turns out a whole story: a prelude to *Tristan* that is a miracle of continuous melody without end, even though—seemingly—there isn't a tune anywhere in it. Do you begin to see what I mean by understanding melody in a different way? The *Tristan* prelude is one long, passionate melody for almost ten minutes. That certainly is a lot of melody for a composer who is supposed to be unmelodic! But, you see, his melody grows out of little scraps—those motives at the beginning; and that's where people make the mistake of thinking there is no melody in Wagner.

Of course, what makes it even more difficult for people to recognize the melody is that frightening word *counterpoint*, which means, as you know, more than one melody going on at the same time. That really gets in people's way; but it shouldn't, because after all, the more melody the better. And counterpoint can be terribly exciting. For example, in this same *Tristan* prelude, much later on, Wagner builds a hair-raising climax by using counterpoint in this way: the strings are pouring out *their* melody, climbing higher and higher, in a frenzy:

And while that frenzy is going on, the horns and cellos, down lower, are screaming out the first four-note motive we heard over and over:

And that's not all. At the same time, the trumpet joins in with all his force, right in the middle, between the other two melodies, singing the *second* four-note motive, again and again:

211

Now do you think that is too much melody for a human
ear to catch all at once? Here it is put together and I'd
make a bet that you can hear it all—every note:

What a climax that is—one of the most thrilling ever
composed! And yet it's counterpoint, that frightening
word, that makes some people afraid to listen to Bach
fugues, or to Wagner operas. But don't you ever be scared
of counterpoint. Counterpoint is not an absence of melody, it's an abundance of melody; it doesn't erase melody,
it multiplies it.

And now to make this idea still clearer, we're going
to look at parts of a movement from a Mozart symphony,
the first movement of his great *G-minor symphony*, which
will illustrate everything we've been talking about so far.
The beautiful theme that opens this movement is a perfect example of the 1-2-3 method we learned about before. First, there's a phrase:

—second, he repeats the same phrase, slightly lower:

—and third, the takeoff:

Certainly nobody will quarrel with *that* as being unmelodic; it has such a beautiful shape and arch. That's another important feature of a good melody—its shape—the curve it makes, as it rises with tension, and settles down in relaxation. And this Mozart theme is a perfectly shaped melody.

But in the course of the movement, as the theme is being developed, there are all kinds of places that might be called unmelodic, or at least less melodic. But even those places *are* melodic, as much as the main theme is, if you just listen to them correctly. For instance, you'll notice that the very first two notes of the main theme:

—form a little motive by themselves, just as in Wagner—a motive that is used all through the movement. For instance, about halfway along, one part of the orchestra is playing with the motive, this way:

—while the strings are playing in counterpoint the same two-note motive, only stretched out in long notes:

—so that together, it makes this wonderful sound:

And that's all made out of those first little two notes! So you see, it's all pure melody, even the development parts. The same is true of this seemingly unmelodic section:

Some people would say that passage lacks melody; but the theme is right there, only it's down in the bass instruments:

—while on top, there is exciting counterpoint going on, as in a Bach fugue:

You just have to learn to listen for melody in the depths of music, as well as on top. And if you do, how different music will sound to you!

What's even harder is to hear melody that's neither on top nor on the bottom, but in the middle, sort of like a sandwich. Here's one place you should be on the lookout for, where again the little motive is being developed on top, over motionless notes on the bottom:

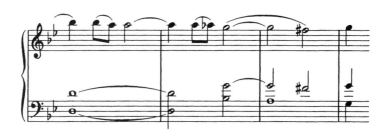

But in the middle, two clarinets are having *their* say about the motive:

And they're so sweet and tender that it would be a shame if you missed them. It would be like having two pieces of dry bread without anything in between them. Listen to the whole sandwich now, top slice, bottom slice and clarinet filling:

So *that's* all melody, too.

Our main question has been "What is a melody?" Well, what is it? Have we found out yet? Any series of notes, we said before. But that's not a satisfying answer because some series of notes please us and others don't. So I guess the question ought to be: "What makes an *unmelody?*" So far we've discussed a few of the reasons why some people find certain kinds of music unmelodic: like melodies going against each other, as they do in counterpoint; or a melody singing away down in the bass, not easily recognized; or buried in the middle of a sandwich which is hard to find; or a melody constructed out of tiny motives, which is not exactly a tune. But the really important reason—and I guess this is what I've been coming to all this time—is the question of what our ears expect: in other words, taste. And that, in turn, depends on what our ears are used to hearing.

For instance, you may now understand how important repetition is in making a melody easy to latch on to. O.K.—but what happens when we hear melodies that don't repeat at all, that just weave on and on, always new? It's true that we usually like them less, *at first.* But that doesn't mean they're any less melodic; in fact, the farther away you get from that kind of "Mack the Knife" repetition, the harder the melodies may get to latch on to, but also the nobler and more beautiful they can become. Some of the really greatest melodies ever written are of this kind, nonrepeating long lines; only they're not necessarily the ones people go around whistling in the streets.

For instance, I remember so well the day my piano teacher brought me a new piece to study, when I was fourteen years old or so, which was Bach's *Italian Concerto;* and when I began to read the second movement, with its long, ornamental melody line, I simply couldn't understand it. It just seemed to wander around, with no place to go. Maybe you know it?

Andante

And so it goes weaving on, spinning out that long golden thread, never once repeating itself for almost five minutes. Do you find it wandering and aimless? I find it one of the glories of all music, now today; but I didn't think so when I was fourteen. I was still young enough to think that every melody had to be a repeating *tune*, because that's what my brief musical experience had taught my ears to expect.

In exactly the same way that our tastes change with growing up and hearing all kinds of music, so people's tastes change from one period of history to another. The melodies people loved in Beethoven's time would have shocked and startled the people of Bach's time, one hundred years earlier, and I'm equally sure that some of

today's modern music, which people complain about as ugly and unmelodic, will be perfectly charming everyday stuff to the people of tomorrow.

Let us look at an example, another long, nonrepeating melodic line, by the great modern German composer Paul Hindemith. Hindemith wrote this melody almost forty years ago, in a piece called *Concert Music for Strings and Brass;* and I suppose there are still people who call this unmelodic, even after forty years. I consider it one of the most moving and beautifully shaped melodies, not only of modern music, but of all music; and I have a feeling that you'll agree with me:

Whether you like that or not, *that* is a great melodic line, and there are four minutes of these beautiful curves, arches, peaks and valleys. And if there are any of you who did not like it, who found it unmelodic, awkward, or graceless, let me comfort you by saying that those were just the words used eighty years ago about another German composer named Brahms.

These days, when we think of melody, we almost immediately think of Brahms; but there *was* a time when people complained bitterly about his music as being totally lacking in melody. To show you how careful you have to be in deciding what is a melody and what isn't, look at the last movement of Brahms' *Fourth Symphony*— an extraordinary movement for many reasons, but chiefly for the reason that its main theme is nothing but a scale of six notes:

—plus two notes to finish it off:

—eight notes in all, one to a bar:

Allegro energico e passionato

And following those eight bars come thirty variations, each one also eight bars long, and each one containing those same eight simple notes, always in the same key.

And that, plus a short windup at the end, is the whole movement. Now, that doesn't sound very promising in terms of melody, does it—a scale and a cadence? And yet, what Brahms gives us in this movement is a work of such glowing, fiery *melodic* beauty as to leave us cheering. How does he do it? In all the ways we've learned about: counterpoint, motives, repetitions, the 1-2-3 method, theme in the bass, theme in the middle, the whole lot. But I'm not going to explain it any further because I think that by this time you're prepared to listen to this so-called unmelodic work of Brahms and hear it for the magnificent outpouring of *melody* that it really is. And if you're still wondering: "What is a melody?" just follow this movement sometime on a recording and you'll realize that melody is exactly what a great composer wants it to be—nothing more or less.

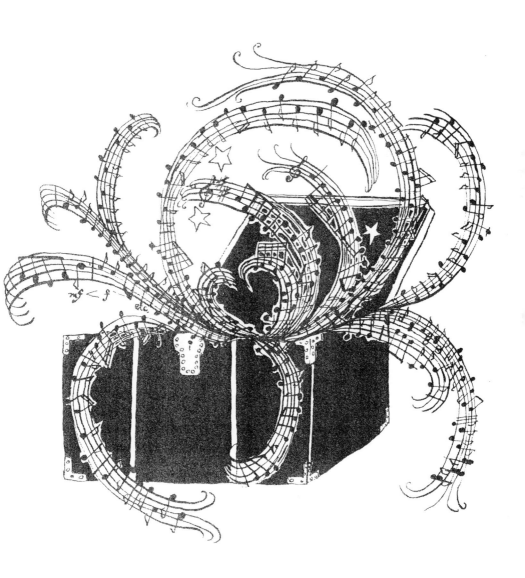

*W*hat Is Sonata Form?

Let's dig into that terrifying old thing called Sonata Form. I've avoided the subject for years, not so much because it's difficult, but because so many words have already been spilled about it in so many music appreciation classes, where sonata form often winds up sounding like a road map with a lot of strange names like "Exposition" and "Recapitulation" and whatnot. But I hope that by the end of this chapter, the idea of sonata form is going to have much more meaning for you than that.

Let's start out by exploring the first movement of the last symphony by Mozart, the one known as the *Jupiter*. But, you may wonder, why talk about a *symphony* when I said we were going to be looking at *sonatas?* Well, the answer to that one is easy; a symphony *is* a sonata.[1] You see, a sonata is a piece usually in several movements, that has a certain basic musical form; and when that form is used in a piece for a *solo* instrument, like a piano, or

225

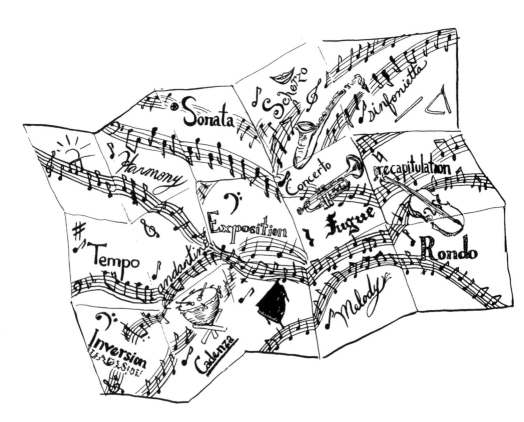

violin or flute, or even a solo instrument with piano accompaniment, the piece is called a sonata.

When the *same* form is used in a piece for three instruments, it's called a trio; and for four instruments it's called a quartet; for five, a quintet, and so on. But when this form is used in a piece for a full orchestra, it's called a symphony. Simple. A symphony is merely a sonata for orchestra. And that's all I'm going to tell you for the moment. Here's the very beginning:

226

The thing that interests us most about this movement, for our immediate purposes, is its form, its musical shape. The shape of a musical composition is the hardest thing for most people to grasp. They can remember a tune or a rhythm easily enough, even harmonies and counterpoints. But the *form* is harder to understand because grasping the form of a piece means seeing it all at once— or, I should say, hearing it all at once—which is, of course, impossible since music takes place in *time* instead of in space. So how can you hear it all at once?

You can see the form of a painting, or a church, more or less all at once because their forms exist in space. When you look at the stage of Philharmonic Hall,[2] for instance, you see its whole form instantly and you can take pleasure in its proportions and its balances.

But with a piece of music, you actually *hear* form. And it takes *time* to hear the form. You have to keep in your head all the notes you've already heard while you're lis-

227

tening to the new ones, so that by the time the piece is over, it all adds up to one continuous form. Maybe that sounds impossible, but it's not. Of course, it's not easy, either. But if you know a little about the form in *advance*—for instance, if you know the piece is going to be in *sonata* form—it all becomes much easier, because you can almost predict what musical shapes are going to happen. That's what we're going to do now, by finding out what a sonata is.

This word *sonata* originally meant simply a piece of music. It comes form the Latin word *sonare*, "to sound." A *sonata* is anything that is *sounded* by instruments, as opposed to a *cantata*, which is anything that is *sung* (from the Latin word *cantare*, "to sing").

But it's only in the last two hundred years or so that the word *sonata* has acquired a special meaning, which describes the form of a piece, and in particular, the first movement of the piece. In a classical sonata the other movements could be in a number of other forms, but the opening movement had to be in what we call sonata form. And this first movement form laid the foundations of the symphony as we have known it from that time (almost two hundred years ago), right on into our own twentieth century. You can see how important it is that we know what the basic classical form is, the form of the first movement of a sonata.

How to explain this immense popularity and growth of sonata form over two centuries? What makes it so satisfying, so complete? Two things really: first, its perfect three-part balance, and second, the excitement of its contrasting elements. Balance and contrast: in these two words we have the main secrets of sonata form.

Let's consider first that three-part design, something we can see all around us. Think of a bridge with two

great towers rising on either side of the river, and the connecting span sweeping over the water between them. That's a three-part form. You must all have felt the pleasure and satisfaction that come from looking at such a structure. Or think of an elm tree, with its central trunk, and the umbrella-shaped branches arching out on both sides. Or the three-part balance of a human face, with its centerpiece of nose and mouth, and its two mirror-like sidepieces of eyes and ears. All examples of three-part form: one, two, three.

Of course, any form as basic and natural as that must be just as natural in music. And so it is; the most basic form of a simple song is usually a three-part form. Take for instance the old nursery tune that we all know as "Twinkle, Twinkle, Little Star." There's a first part, which we'll call A:

Twink - le, twink-le, lit - tle star, How I won-der what you are.

Then comes a middle part, which we'll call B:

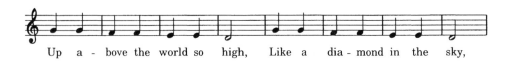

Up a - bove the world so high, Like a dia - mond in the sky,

And finally we return to the first part, A again, and the song is over:

Twink - le, twink-le, lit - tle star, How I won-der what you are.

There you have a clear, exact three-part form: A, B, A.

Let's see how this simple little construction grows in size when it's used in a slightly longer song form. In fact, most pop tunes stick to this A-B-A pattern very strictly. The only difference here (and this is important, as you'll see later) is that usually the first A section is repeated right away, before the B section comes. So the pattern is really A-A-B-A, instead of just A-B-A. But it's still made out of those same three parts, A-B-A, only the first part is played twice in a row. Let's take a pop tune, in fact, a typical Beatles tune called "And I Love Her," and see what happens. First there is an A section:

230

I give her all my love,— That's all I do;—

And if you saw my love You'd love her too,— I— love her.—

Then that A section is repeated exactly the same:

She gives me ev- 'ry - thing, *etc.*

—and so on. The repeated A. Now comes the contrast-ing B section:

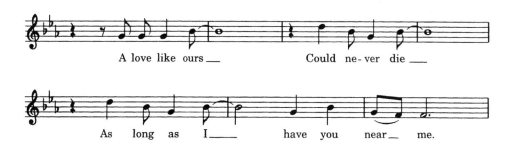

A love like ours— Could ne- ver die —

As long as I— have you near— me.

—which brings us back again to the A section in all its glory:

Bright are the stars that shine, *etc.*

231

So it goes, right to the end of the piece.

Well, that's a small step forward from "Twinkle, Twinkle, Little Star," but it's a step. It's grown in size, and it has that extra deluxe feature, the repeat of the first A section, which "Twinkle, Twinkle" does not. Let's follow the growth of a three-part song even further, as it expands into a big operatic aira—for example, the famous aria from the opera *Carmen* that is sung by the other woman of the opera, Micaela. This is a little more complicated, or let's say, sophisticated. It doesn't break up quite so neatly into an exact A-B-A, but I'm sure you'll be able to follow its three parts just as easily as the Beatles song. The sweet, lyrical first part:[3]

—the more excited and dramatic middle part:

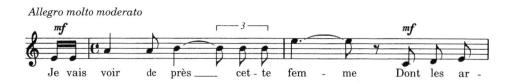

232

ti - fi - ces mau - dits   Ont fi - ni   par fai - re un in - fâ - me   *etc.*

—and the return again to the quiet first part:³

Je   dis,⎯⎯ que rien ne m'é - pou - van - te,

Now that you have learned to recognize a three-part song form, I think we're ready to take the plunge into sonata form itself. This is because a typical sonata movement is really only a more expanded version of a three-part song form, even to the balancing of its two A sections on either side of the central B section. Here's where those nasty road map names come in: the first part, or A section, is called the *Exposition.* This is where the themes of the movement are stated for the first time, or *exposed,* if you will. This is then followed by the B section, in which one or some of all of those themes are developed in different ways; and so it is called the *Development* section. Finally, just as you expected, we get the A section stated again; and this third part is usually called— watch out!—the *Recapitulation.*

Wow; that's a tough one. Actually, I'm not too crazy about any of these words myself, but what can we do? We have to use the words that are most commonly used in order to be understood; so I guess we're stuck with those words, Exposition, Development, and Recapitulation, for our A-B-A. But whatever words we use, the *idea* of the three parts is still clear and simple: the feeling of balance we get from two similar sections, A and A, situated on either side of the development, just as the ears are situated in a balancing position to the nose.

But I said earier that there were *two* main secrets to the sonata: balance *and* contrast. This idea of contrast is just as important as the other. It's what gives the sonata form its drama and excitement. How does this contrast take place? Here's where we're going to have to get technical for a minute or two, because what I'm going to show you now is very important; in fact, this is the root of this whole sonata business. And that is the sense of *key*, of tonality.

Most music that we hear is written in one *key* or another. Not so much the concert music that is written these days, but most of the music you're likely to hear, is in a key. You've all had the experience of singing a song that felt uncomfortable to your voice, and wishing it could be lower or higher. What you're really wishing for is a lower or higher key. For instance, the Beatles' song I played before is in the key of E-flat major. (See the example on p. 231.) But it could also be in G-major:

—or in C-major:

—or in any of twelve different major keys. (Not twelve others, but twelve in all.) But whatever key it's in, let's say C-major, you feel a *key-note*, a center, or home plate,

where the music belongs, starts out from, and gets back
to. That center is called the *tonic* and the tonic *note* is
the first note of the scale:

—and the tonic *chord* is the chord you build on to that
note:

All the other notes of the scale also have names; but
I won't bother you with them except for this one, which
I'd like you to remember: the *dominant*. That's the name
given to the fifth note of any scale, and in this key of C
major the fifth note is G.

—and the *dominant chord* is built on that note:

Now come the main event, how these two key centers,
the tonic and the dominant, relate to each other. If I
play a tonic and a dominant chord, in that order, what
do you feel?

235

Something is left unfinished, unresolved, isn't it? You feel a desperate urge to get back to the tonic, where you started, don't you? Okay, let's play them in reverse order, dominant to tonic:

Now you feel satisfied, don't you? So you see, a tonic is like a magnet; you can pull away from it, going to other chords, other keys, or tonal centers; but in the end the tonic always pulls you back irresistibly:

Out of this magnetic pull, away from and back to the tonic, classical sonata form is built. That's where the drama, the tension lies, in the contrast of keys. Let's see how this works in an actual piece of music, again by Mozart. The composer will naturally begin his sonata in the key of the tonic. His opening theme will be in that key, as in this famous Mozart *Piano Sonata in C Major*, K. 545:

But now, like a magician, he begins to lure us away
from the tonic to a new key, the dominant:

There we are in the dominant key: G major. And in this
new key Mozart gives us a new theme, his second theme:

237

Then finally, still in the key of G major, he gives us a
little fanfare-like tune with which he closes the exposition:

Fanfare

—solidly established in the dominant key of G major.
The exposition part of this movement is over.

At this point in the classical sonata we usually bump
smack into a repeat sign, which means go back to the
beginning and play that whole A section, or exposition,
you have just heard, all over again. Just like the Beatles
song. Remember? A-A-B-A. And so for the second time,
we hear the full exposition: first theme, second theme,
closing theme, starting in the tonic and winding up in
the dominant.

Actually, this whole exposition has been like the first
act of a drama about running away from home—pulling
away from that force called the tonic. The next act coming up, the development, intensifies that drama, wandering even faster away from home, through even more
distant keys, but then finally giving in and coming home
in the third act, or recapitulation. It's as though we were
trying to roam, to explore, escape, be free; but always
there is that magnet sitting there, pulling us back. That's
the drama of it all. Therefore, in the second part, or
development section, of this Mozart sonata, the composer lets his imagination roam free. The themes he has
stated in the exposition wander around in one foreign
key after another, like a trip to various other countries.

But because this particular *C Major Sonata* of Mozart is a very short one, the development is also very short. In fact, the only theme Mozart does develop is that little fanfare in the closing theme of the exposition. But now, in the development, he puts it through its paces, like this:

—which brings us to the third and last section of this three-part sonata form, the recapitulation.

In most classical sonatas, this is the moment when that magnet we were talking about finally wins out and draws us back home, to the tonic; and the whole exposition is repeated or *recapitulated*. Only in this third section of the recapitulation (which is basically the same music as the exposition), we never leave the tonic key.

Even the second theme and the closing theme, which we originally heard in the dominant, are not allowed to wander away into the dominant. This time we must hear *all* of it in the *tonic*, the original key. When the movement is over we are safely at home in C major where we began, and all that drama of pulling away from the magnet is finished.

Of course, Mozart, like all geniuses, is full of surprises. He doesn't always play the game according to the rules.[4] In fact he often gives us more musical pleasure by breaking rules than by obeying them. In this same C *Major Sonata*, where the recapitulation *should* be in the tonic key of C, Mozart holds out on us. He is still resisting that magnet of the tonic as he gives us the recapitulation in the unexpected key of F:

etc.

Then Mozart gives in, and the magnet wins out after all. The rest of this little movement is all safe and warm, back home in C major:

—and the movement is over.

That wasn't too terribly hard to follow, was it? (Although it's terribly hard to play. It sounds much easier than it actually is.) But it's not very hard to follow the form. Do you see now what I mean by balance and contrast? The balance of the three-part form: Exposition, Development, Recapitulation, and the contrast of the tonic with the dominant. Of course there's much more to it than we can explain here: the contrasting key is not always the dominant; rules get broken right and left. Then there's the whole business of introductions and

241

codas, extra sections at the beginning and end of a sonata movement. You've got plenty of time to learn about all those, but none of it changes the basic form. What matters now is that you see the two main things: the magnetic effect of the tonic and the A-B-A form. Armed with only that information, you should be able to recognize and follow any classical sonata form movement.

Just to see if I'm right, consider the last movement of a twentieth-century piece: Prokofieff's *Classical Symphony*, a deliciously spoofing imitation of the eighteenth-century classical sonata form. It has an exposition, consisting of a first theme in the tonic:

—the second theme in the dominant:

—and the closing theme in the dominant:

Then that whole exposition is repeated exactly; followed by a development section, in which these themes are tossed around; and then the recapitulation, which is the whole exposition again, only in the tonic. It is a perfect

242

example: Sonata form at its simplest and clearest: A-A-B-A.

I hope that you will try to listen to Prokofieff's *Classical Symphony* and that you'll be able to follow the form of this last movement. If I am right, you are well on your way toward being a real music listener. As I said before, anyone can hear and enjoy a tune or a rhythm. That's easy. But a true listener hears much more. That listener hears the *form* of a piece, just as clearly as he or she sees the three-part form of a bridge. If any of you still have doubts, then try, try again; and soon, with your new ears, you too will have the pleasure of hearing musical form.

$\mathscr{A}$ Tribute to Sibelius

A month ago, President Lyndon Johnson officially recognized 1965 as Sibelius Year. This is in observance of the one hundredth anniversary of the birth of the composer Jean Sibelius; and so we join the whole world in honoring the memory of this great man from Finland.

Sibelius was a great and strange kind of genius, but perhaps the best way to begin to understand him is by listening to his most famous single composition, *Finlandia*. It's famous not only for musical reasons, although for a short work it is musicaly very stirring and passionate, indeed. But what underlies the music is another kind of passion: the passion of patriotism. At the time Sibelius wrote *Finlandia*, around 1900, his country was not free. Its government was controlled by Czarist Russia, and its cultural life was still mostly dominated by its other neighbor, Sweden. In fact, all educated and literary people in Finland had for centuries spoken not Finnish, but Swedish. The old Finnish language was considered to be vulgar, a language for peasants.

But during the nineteenth century this language of the people began slowly to be accepted and to acquire a dignity of its own. The ancient Finnish epics and sagas began to be regarded as important literature, not just provincial folk tales. The people began to be proud of their poetry, their old folk songs, their own national heritage. All these things were signs of a revolution that was boiling up under the surface: a *double* revolution, against Swedish culture on the one hand, and Russian political power on the other.

This *Finlandia*, by Sibelius, like many other pieces of his, was a part of that national revolution. In fact, it proved to be so exciting to the Finnish audiences, with its warlike rhythms and its inspiring, hymn-like middle part, that for a while the czarist government forbade performances of it, especially during periods of political upheaval. It was like dynamite. Even so, it had its first performance in 1900 by the Helsinki Philharmonic, and we are told that it did more to bring about Finnish independence finally than a thousand speeches and pamphlets.

To the Finnish people, the abstract symphonies of Sibelius are filled with just as much patriotic feeling as *Finlandia.* The *Second Symphony in D,* in particular, is for them and for many people all over the world a masterpiece that carries the meaning of freedom, the triumph over oppression. This is partly because the music sounds so deeply nationalistic. Not that Sibelius uses actual Finnish themes or folk songs. He himself once said that he never used a single real Finnish folk song in any of his music. But somehow his themes *sound* like folk songs. They sound Finnish and they seem to grow out of the Finnish language itself.

246

But there's much more to a Sibelius symphony than just nationalism. The special fascination of such music comes from the suspense in its construction. As in a great detective story, Sibelius plants clues for you right from the beginning, clues that point the way. These clues sometimes may puzzle you, but they always keep you eager for the next one. In the end they all link up, so that when the light finally dawns, and all is made clear, you feel the thrill of having solved a great mystery, you the listener.

I can give you some idea how this works by tracing only one single thread of the tangled mystery through

the course of the symphony's four movements. The thread I have in mind is simply a string of three notes, in their ascending order of the scale, like this:

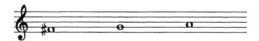

Couldn't be simpler. His clue of three notes is planted immediately at the beginning of the first movement, as an accompaniment idea, sort of a "vamp-'til-ready." It sounds like this:

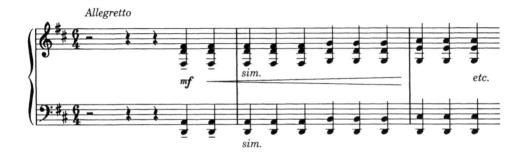

Over that accompaniment figure appears the first main theme. Lo and behold, it too is built out of three notes of the scale, only in *descending* order, like "Three Blind Mice," as if contradicting the first clue:

Here is the accompaniment, with the theme on top of it:

248

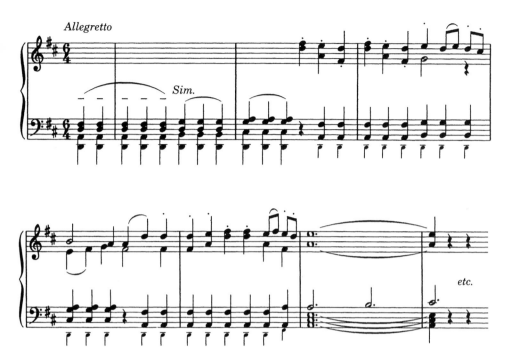

Obviously Sibelius is trying to tell us something with these two related but contradictory clues. Maybe what he is trying to tell us is that perhaps a solution of this complicated mystery case can be found by investigating a few simple notes of the everyday scale. It seems crazy. Maybe it's impossible. But let's find out by following our thread of clues further, each one of them being a version of those first three scale notes, whether upwards or downwards, repeated or rearranged or expanded, or whatever. For instance, later on in this first movement the notes are played on plucked strings, growing from three to five notes, from soft to loud, expanding, like a rising flock of birds, like this:

Then suddenly these same notes *double* in speed, buzzing away like a gigantic swarm of insects:

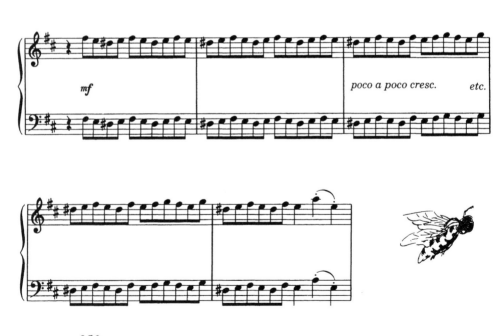

All that's made out of those same three little old notes. In fact, throughout the first movement, those three innocent scale notes keep turning up in a hundred different disguises, and it happens in all four movements. For instance, the main theme of the second movement features those same rising scale notes, four of them this time:

What's more, this theme is played over other scale notes, descending ones in the cellos:

It's amazing how many different ways those few scale notes can be manipulated by a genius like Sibelius. The third movement, the scherzo, turns the same notes into a savage roar by jumbling them up, just three of them, and playing them as fast as possible:

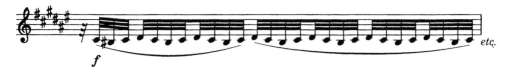

Imagine, that wild sound is only another disguise of the original three scale notes, only whirled up into a storm.

251

This one thread of clues we've been tracing goes through disguise after disguise: brooding, fierce, gentle, playful. At last we reach the last movement, which is ushered in by a brave trumpet theme, made in the simplest way, out of the original three notes:

At last it seems as though we're nearing our solution of the mystery: it's clear and affirmative. But hold on, we must still go through one more disguise, perhaps the most impressive one of the whole symphony. It's where the scale notes turn into a mournfully haunting, folk-like tune in the minor:

This little tune repeats hypnotically over and over, while underneath it the scale notes, the same ones as before, writhe about like a great serpent, also repeating again and again:

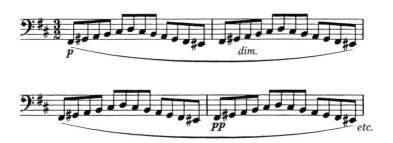

As the scale notes go on writhing this way and that, they gradually accumulate more and more power, more and more sound, until finally they gain the strength to burst out into a major tonality. The brave music is heard again, leading to an ending that is almost overpowering. At last we have the solution toward which all these scaley-clues have been leading. You may find different meanings in the ending:

the rejoicing after a storm,

the joy of climbing a mountain and reaching the top,

the joy of winning a game

or passing a tough exam

or being well after a sickness.

But to the people of Finland this ending will always mean one thing only: freedom!

$\mathcal{M}$usical Atoms:
A Study of Intervals

 In a previous chapter, we started off with a single note. Well, here is another one. Play it on your piano and it can be a pretty sound:

But is it music? Not at all. One simple note by itself is not music—not even a molecule of music, not even an atom. A single note is more like a single proton or an electron, which, as you know, are meaningless all by themselves. You need at least one of each—at least two atomic particles—in order to create an atom. And in exactly the same way you need at least two notes before you can begin to have an atom of music. Because with that one lonely note, isolated, nothing is happening. It's just floating in space. But once you have two notes:

—you suddenly feel a relationship between them, like an electrical tension. There is already the beginning of a musical meaning. And with *three* notes, that meaning increases:

—and before you know it:

We've got "The Blue Danube."

You see what has happened: those musical protons and electrons (the separate notes, that is) have combined together, forming atoms, which have then combined into molecules, which have finally combined into recognizable matter— like the baton I conduct with—or your own head of hair, or that example of

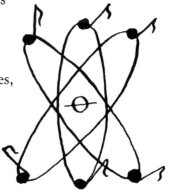

256

the "Blue Danube Waltz." So it turns out that an atom of music is not a single note at all, as you might think, but at least *two* notes. That two-note relationship is called an *Interval.* A very important word, "interval," because it is the heart and soul of music. Music is not made out of single notes by themselves, but rather out of the intervals *between* one note and another. That's why it is so necessary for us to understand this word *interval.*

Everyone knows the word in daily speech as meaning a span of time between two events. For instance, they say in the British theatres, "Between Acts I and II, there will be an *interval* of fifteen minutes," by which they mean an intermission. So an interval usually means a measurement of time.

In music, of course, we measure time by breaking it up into rhythms and meters and bars and tempos. But we also measure other things in music—especially *pitches,* those separate notes we just mentioned. And that's how we use the word *interval* in music: to measure the distance between one note and another.

Now how do we do this? Let's say we think of all the pitches there are, marked out on a long measuring tape, that reads from zero to infinity:

—zero being any low note, and infinity being those high, high notes that only dogs can hear. Let's section off this tape in feet—one foot, two feet, three feet, and so on— each foot being that lowest note repeated over and over again, but at a higher and higher pitch. For instance, we could take C as our lowest note, our "zero" mark on the tape:

—and as we unreel one foot of tape we arrive at the next C:

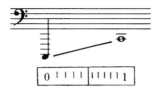

Another foot on the reel brings us to the next:

—and so on all the way up:

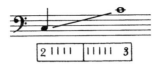

258

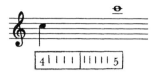

Each of those sections, one foot long apiece, is equal to what musicians call an *octave,* which comes from the Latin word *octo* meaning eight. This is because there are eight scale tones beginning on any note and ending with its next highest appearance:

That's a span of eight notes. (See Chapter Fourteen, pages 288–90.) And that span of an octave—

—is called an interval. And any smaller section within that octave is also called an interval. If it spans seven notes:

—it will be called a Seventh.

If it spans six notes:

—it's a Sixth, and so on. If it covers only two notes:

—it's called a Second.

Actually, the intervals go on even beyond the octave: there's a Ninth:

a Tenth:

—and so on. But for our purposes let's just stay inside our one little octave, one foot of the measuring tape. Now don't forget: these intervals don't always have to start on the *first* note of the scale:

They can start anywhere. I can begin somewhere inside the octave, let's say on E:

—and span three notes up to G:

That also makes an interval of a Third. Or from that G:

—up *four* notes to C:

—makes a Fourth.

Of course these intervals don't always have to go up. They can be descending as well as ascending. That interval of the Fourth just mentioned:

—can be turned upside down, into a descending Fourth:

261

It's the same interval, only backwards. And, in fact, intervals don't have to be either ascending *or* descending. They can be simultaneous, the two notes played together:

That's the same Fourth, only a simultaneous one. And here's a simultaneous Third:

—and a Second:

Now this is interesting. We're getting away from *melody,* where notes follow each other in time:

—and into the new region of *harmony,* where notes sound at the *same* time:

These simultaneous intervals are the stuff of which *chords* are made. You take that Fourth just given:

—and add another note to it:

—and you've got a *chord:*

So you see, intervals work both ways, horizontally (one note after the other), which means *melodically;* and vertically (both notes at once), which means *harmonically.* That's very important to remember; because if you understand that point, there is nothing in music you won't be able to understand.

Let me give you a tiny example of how this horizontal–vertical thing actually works. Here is a set of intervals, all of them descending Seconds:

Horizontal, melodic intervals. Now here is that set of intervals three times, each time with different *vertical* intervals underneath, that is, different harmony. I'm sure you'll recognize immediately how the musical meaning of that set changes each time:

If that sounds familiar to you, it should. It's the pattern of the song "Help!" as sung by the Beatles:

Moderato

Help me if you can. I'm feel-ing down___ And I do_

___ ap-pre-ci-ate___ you be-ing 'round___

Help me get___ my feet back on the ground___

There's only one other thing you should know before you can really appreciate intervals, whether it be music by the Beatles or by Brahms, and that is the idea of *Inversion*, the inverting of intervals. This is a bit tricky, so pay close attention. To invert something means to turn it upside down or backward. You would think that to invert an interval—let's say, this *ascending* Third:

265

—would mean simply to play it backwards:[1]

—a _descending_ Third. But that's not what inversion means at all. To invert an interval you may play the two notes either forward or backward as you choose, _but in the opposite direction._ Does that seem too hard? It isn't really. Here are the same two notes:

(E)

—an _ascending_ Third. Now, we invert that interval[2] by playing the same two notes, _in the same order_, only descending:

(E)

What has happened? It's not a Third anymore! The interval has changed into a Sixth. What was a Third is now a Sixth—the same notes, only inverted. Now suppose we had started with the same interval, only descending:

(C)

To invert _that_, again we play the same two notes, _in the same order_, but this time _ascending_:

(C)

267

And again, it's turned into a Sixth.

What does this mean? Simply that whenever you invert an interval, it becomes a *different* interval. And, by the way, the new interval, the inverted one, can always be discovered by subtracting the original one from the number 9. Isn't that an amazing fact? As we just saw, a Third inverts to a Sixth; and 3 from 9 leaves 6. In the same way, a Second:

—inverts to a Seventh:

2 from 9 is 7. And a Fourth:

—will invert to a Fifth:

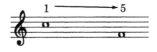

—because 4 from 9 is 5. And vice versa. A Fifth will invert to a Fourth, a Sixth to a Third, and a Seventh to a Second. Get it?

Again, by the way, these interval–inversions don't necessarily have to be made of the same notes. *Any* Fifth can be said to be the inversion of any *Fourth*. For example, this Fifth:

—is an inversion of this Fourth:

Now: let's take the big jump from the Beatles to Brahms and see what all this has to do, for example, with the first movement of Brahms' *Fourth Symphony.*[3] Just this: that Brahms, great master that he was, built almost the whole movement out of the interval of the Third, and its inversion, the interval of the Sixth. It's astonishing how Brahms does it. Let me show you a sample or two. The beautiful main theme, right at the beginning, starts off the movement with a descending Third:

And it's immediately answered by its inversion, an ascending Sixth:

Again comes a descending Third:

—and again an ascending Sixth:

What's even more fascinating about the construction of this intervallic theme is that each interval begins exactly a Third below where the previous interval finished! Just look—the opening Third:

—and then, a Third still lower starts the answering Sixth:

Then, a Third below *that,* begins the next interval of the Sixth:

Then again a Third below *that* the next Sixth begins:

A marvel of construction!

All this is very fascinating as a mechanical exercise in building-blocks or something; but does it make beautiful music? Well, just play this on your piano:

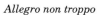

Quite promising, isn't it? And that's just four little bars of music! Now of course Brahms can't just stick to Thirds and Sixths forever. In the next phrase, he expands the descending interval to an octave:

Then again a rising Third:

Again an octave:

271

—and again a Third:

Then, as he goes on developing his theme, other intervals come into play: Fourths, Seconds and whatnot. But the important thing is that the beginning of that theme, those first four bars, out of which the whole movement is going to be made, is all intervals of the Third and its inversion, the Sixth.

Now let's jump ahead to the next theme in this movement; and what do we find? Again it's almost entirely built on Thirds:

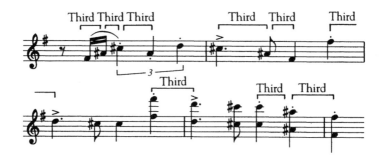

Incredible! But as this theme goes on, we begin to feel something's wrong, that suddenly there are no Thirds at all:

Ah, but on closer inspection, it turns out that the *accompaniment* to that tune, underneath, is nothing *but a*

series of descending Thirds (and what's more, they're descending by intervals of the Third):

Isn't that lucky? And isn't it typical of Brahms, the master builder? Here are that theme and accompaniment to-gether:

And so all through this movement—exposition, devel-opment, recapitulation, coda and all—we come upon these intervals of Thirds and Sixths used in the most ingenious ways, horizontally and vertically, upside down and inside out.

273

Perhaps all this stuff about intervals is technical; for composers and professional musicians, not for the ordinary listener. But I can't tell you how helpful it is for a plain untechnical music lover to know about intervals. They come up all the time in conversation. You hear people speak of harmonizing in Thirds, singing in octaves, and so on. Therefore, knowing the intervals gives you a language, or terminology, in which to talk to one another about music. After all, didn't we decide that the interval is the *atom* of all music? What can be more important, or more basic, than that? So let's forge ahead and get to know intervals better.

Remember that measuring tape we used before to mark off the octaves? Well, let's now consider just one octave—that is, one foot of the tape. What a lucky coincidence: it's marked off into twelve inches, and there also happen to be exactly twelve notes in an octave! Now I don't want to confuse you. I know I said before that an octave has *eight* notes in it (which is why it's called an octave); but then I was speaking of our regular major scale, which uses only *some* of the notes that exist in an octave. For instance, the C-major scale, as you know, uses only the white notes—eight of them. But there are black ones too. So all in all there are exactly twelve different notes in every octave, each one exactly the same distance from its neighbor. With the thirteenth we're back again where we started. (See the keyboard illustration on page 185. Also Chapter Fourteen on modes.)

Now the distance between any two neighboring notes is, as you know, a Second. But, as you may *not* know, it is a *minor* Second. A minor Second is the smallest distance we can move from one note to the next, in our Western musical system. Take note of that word "West-

ern," because our music—European and American—is not the only music in the world by any means. There are lots of other systems—Hindu music, for instance—which divide the octave differently, not just into twelve equal parts. But we Westerners are stuck with a musical system based on twelve different tones, like the twelve inches of the foot rule; and these twelve tones are the twelve minor Seconds in the octave:

Now if there is such a thing as a *minor* Second:

Minor 2nd

—there must be a *major* Second as well. And so there is:

Major 2nd

—twice as big an interval as the minor Second. I know this seems to be getting complicated, but I do want you to feel the difference between a minor Second and a major Second, because the piece which we're going to look at now is almost totally made out of themes built on minor and major Seconds, and the difference between them is very important, as you'll see. This hair-raising piece is again a *Fourth Symphony*, this time by the great British composer Ralph Vaughan Williams. Let me show you a bit of what Vaughan Williams does with those tiny intervals in the first movement.

From the very opening bars of the first movement, he is already presenting us with minor Seconds, as if to say: "This is going to be the subject of my symphony":

That's nothing but a descending minor Second:

—followed by the drop of an octave:

Now to build his theme, he repeats that minor Second:

—and follows it up by more minor Seconds, descending from a greater height:

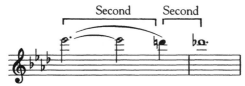

Then, even higher, he gives us two more pairs of descending minor Seconds:

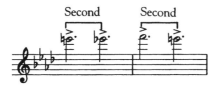

And those four notes—

—form the basic motive, or motto, of the whole symphony.

This motto will occur throughout the whole work,
tossed around in different rhythms, faster and slower. In
the orchestra, this rugged opening theme sounds even
more rugged, because while the high instruments are
playing one note of the interval:

—the low instruments are playing the other:

—and that makes a mighty, clashing dissonance. This
is because when that interval of the minor Second is
played *vertically*—remember?—meaning simultaneously,
it makes harmony of a very bristly kind:

Here is the whole theme now, in all its bite and strength:

Pretty bristly, isn't it?

The very next thing that happens is again made of minor Seconds, only this time rising instead of descending—like a great monster rising out of the sea:

And so it goes. Amazing what you can do with those little Seconds. In fact, all four movements of this symphony exploit that tiny interval to the hilt. For instance,

the next movement uses minor Seconds, in a slow song-like way. Its greatest moment comes just before the end where there is a sad flute solo, mostly made of falling minor Seconds:

But underneath, the harmony in the trombones consists of four very soft chords which, as if by magic, spell out the four-note motto from the first movement:

Here are the flute melody and those chords together in counterpoint—a whole network of minor Seconds:

What a mysterious atmosphere those tiny intervals can make.

Then, abruptly, the third movement charges in, in high spirits, as if to dispel the mystery. But after a brief moment the old four-note motto clangs forth again in the brass, then faster in the woodwinds, and even faster in the strings, as if to show that this riddle of minor Seconds from the first movement is still not solved:

It seems as if all three movements are bent on solving the mystery of those minor Seconds we heard at the beginning. But in the last movement we finally do get

281

the feeling of having solved it, as this great jolly tune breaks in:

Now what is it that makes this music sound so solved, so liberated? It's just this: that after all the messing around with those crabbed little intervals of minor Seconds that we've been hearing for three movements, we finally arrive at a triumphant tune that turns the minor Second into a *major* Second:

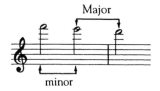

The effect is of a clear, wide-open statement. Now, obviously, major Seconds aren't all that wide open compared, for example, with Fourths or Fifths:

But compared with the scrunchy little *minor* Seconds heard in every conceivable form for three whole move-

282

ments, this major Second seems like the Gates of Heaven itself. Just look at the difference between, let's say, this:

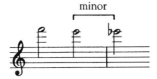

—and this, which is what Vaughan Williams has written:

And there you have the real magic of intervals. In the hands of a composer who's a genius, a modest, humble major Second can have a mountainous majesty.

In the final movement, the interval of the Second is used for all its worth: major and minor, descending and ascending, in all kinds of rhythms—and combined with all the different themes of the Finale in a dazzling display of counterpoint, working itself up into a frenzy of Seconds. But at the very height of this exciting build-up, when everything is going like gangbusters, on the very last page, the composer suddenly hurls us back into the dissonant rage and despair of the opening movement, and with six final hammer blows the symphony comes to a savage end. Why this sudden, brief, angry, dissonant ending after a whole joyful movement that made us feel we had solved something at last? Well, it's as if Vaughan Williams were telling us: "My dear Audience, that's life!"

We've gone about as far as we can, since any further talk would probably be more confusing than clarifying. The next step is to listen to the music by getting a good recording of the Brahms *Fourth* or the Vaughan Williams *Fourth*, or both, and become part of that great universe of musical atoms.

CHAPTER FOURTEEN

*W*hat Is a Mode?

My dear young friends: I am happy and proud to welcome you to our tenth season of Young People's Concerts. Imagine, it's been a whole decade we've been playing and talking about music for you. I don't know how much you've actually learned, but I like to think we must be doing something right, because—well, because it's our tenth season. And to add to the festivities, this is also the first season in which all our programs will be seen on televison *in color,* which is why I've got this modishly colorful tie on.

Which brings us to our subject: "What Is a Mode?" Well, for one thing, musical modes have nothing to do with neckties or dresses, or even with fashions of a musical kind. Modes are simply scales—though not perhaps those same scales you practice on your piano.

They are rather special scales; and I wouldn't have dreamed of bothering you with them, except for an incident that happened a few months ago. My fourteen-year-old daughter Jamie happened to ask me one day why

287

a certain Beatles song had such funny harmony. She couldn't seem to find the right chords for it on her guitar. I began to explain to her that the song was *modal*—that is, it was based on what is called a mode, and I went on to show her the chords that come from it. She got so excited that she wanted to know more and more about it, until finally she said: "Why not tell all this on a Young People's program? Nobody ever heard of modes!" Well, I thought, Jamie is just a natural music lover with the usual weekly piano lesson, and if she finds this material fascinating, why shouldn't you? So here goes, and you can blame it all on Jamie.

All right, then—we already know that a mode is a scale. But, first of all, what is a scale?[1] I'm sure you know; but maybe you've never tried to put it into words. A scale is simply a way of dividing up the distance between any note and the same note repeated an octave higher.

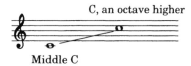

The most famous and often used division of this octave range in our Western music is what we call the *major scale:*

I guess you all know that one. And the other famous one is the *minor scale:*

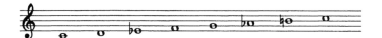

I guess you know that too. Now what's the difference between the major and the minor? Many people think the only difference is that major scales are happy-sounding, and minor ones sound sad. Well, that's sometimes true, but not always. The *real* difference is in the arrangement of the *intervals* into major and minor—you remember how deeply we dug into intervals? (See "Musical Atoms," p. 255.)

You will remember we found that the *smallest* interval—that is, the shortest distance from any one note to its nearest neighbor—is called a half-tone. (It can also be called a "minor second.") From C to C# is a step of a half-tone, and from C# to D is again a half-tone. But from C straight to D is a *whole* tone, since two halves make a whole. Get it? This entire C-major scale is just a series of whole tones and half-tones arranged in a special order. C to D, a whole tone; D to E again a whole tone; E to F, a *half*-tone (since we've skipped nothing); then three whole tones; F to G, G to A, A to B; and finally B to C, a *half*-tone.

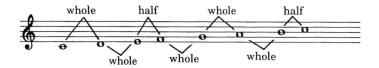

That's the formula for any major scale, whether it begins on C or on E-flat or on Q-sharp: two whole tones, a half-tone, three whole tones, and a half-tone.

The minor scale is almost the same arrangement of intervals, the main difference[2] being in the third note of the scale, which in the minor is a half-tone lower.

289

It doesn't matter whether you start on C or on E-flat or F-sharp, you can always get a major or minor scale by following the same arrangement of intervals. Here is a B-flat major scale:

And here's a B-flat minor scale:

And here's an F-sharp minor scale:

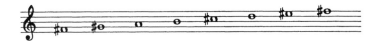

And so it goes. But the important thing to remember is that those two scales—major and minor—*are* modes, which composers of Western music have happened to use more or less exclusively. But they are only *two* modes out of a larger number of possible ones.

Now before I tell you anything else about modes, I'd like to introduce you to a short but marvelous piece, by the great French composer Debussy, a piece completely based on modes that are neither major or minor. This brilliant piece, which is called *Festivals* (or, in French, *Fêtes*), uses all kinds of other modes which, of course, you won't know about yet. You can hear beautiful sounds that will seem a bit strange and ear-tickling. But by the time you finish reading this chapter, you should be able to recognize most of the peculiar things that are going on.

So, for the moment, just imagine a splendid nighttime celebration, with many-colored lights and lanterns everywhere, gorgeous fireworks in the sky. Everyone is dancing

in costumes of long ago. Suddenly, in the middle of the piece, the dance music breaks off, and a procession is heard in the far distance. This march-like music comes nearer and nearer. When it arrives in all its glory, the dance music and the march music are heard together in an exciting blend of tumultuous sounds. Finally, at the end of the piece, it grows late, the crowds thin out—as does the music—and it all ends in a whisper, with an echo or two of the night's festivities hanging in the silent air.

It's an exciting piece, positively goosefleshy. And a lot of the excitement comes from the fact that it uses those strange scales, or modes, which are neither major nor minor. For instance, right at the begining, the driving rhythm of those bright, shining, open intervals of the Fifth way up high tells us that this music is neither major nor minor:

Those empty fifths contain in them neither the third note of the major scale:

—which would turn them into major chords:

—nor the third note of the minor scale, which would turn them into minor chords:

They're just empty, neutral. Soon, underneath them there appears that first swirling dance tune:

—which sounds at first like the usual minor mode. In fact, the first five notes of it are exactly the first five notes of the minor scale:

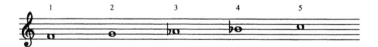

But then comes the twist. The sixth note doesn't belong to any minor scale we know.

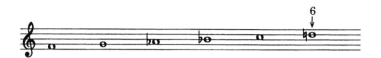

That is where it gets peculiar. But Debussy's tune is shaped just like a scale, isn't it?

What scale is it? Answer: it's the scale of the *Dorian* mode. Don't let that word throw you. Keep calm, sit back, and let's quietly find out just what this Dorian mode is, and why it is so special. The word *Dorian* obviously comes from the Greek;[3] and in fact the Dorian mode, as well as the other modes we're about to discover, does come originally from the music of ancient Greece. We don't know too much about that old Greek music. What we *do* know is that the Greek modes eventually made their way to Rome, where they were taken up by the Roman Catholic Church during the middle ages in a somewhat different form. But the Church kept the old Greek names for the modes: Dorian, Phrygian, Lydian, Mixolydian, Aeolian, Locrian, and Ionian.[4]

That's a mouthful for you, I know. But they're much easier to understand than they are to pronounce; and they are still used today in certain Catholic churches all over the world, in those beautiful chants called plainsong. Here is a tiny example of plainsong, in the Dorian mode:

. Mi - se - re,   -   re   A   -   -   men, Al - le - lu   -   ia

Church chant, in the Dorian mode, using exactly the same scale, the same arrangement of intervals, as Debussy used in his *Fêtes*. But what *is* that scale? Ah, that's easy to discover. To find the Dorian mode on your piano, all you have to do is to start on the note D and play only white notes all the way up to the next D, and you've got it.

Simple. And that's true of all the other Church modes as well: they're all to be found by starting on a given white note and making up a scale *using white notes only*. Isn't that lucky? And we're luckier still with the Dorian mode, because it starts on D, and D is the first letter of

the word *Dorian!* So you have no excuse for forgetting how to find this mode: Dorian, capital D, Dorian, the note D, white notes all the way up, and there is it.

Here's another piece in the Dorian mode. I wonder if you know it:

"Along Comes Mary"[5] is in the ancient and honorable Dorian mode—the same mode we just heard in Debussy and in the plainsong. Who'd have *thunk* it? What is that old Greek mode doing in today's pop music? Well, I'll tell you.

From about the time of Bach until the beginning of our own century—roughly two hundred years—our Western music, as I have already said, has been based almost exclusively on only two modes, the major and the minor. We can't go into the whys and wherefores now, but it's true. Since most of the music we hear in concerts today was written during that two-hundred-year period, we get to think that major and minor modes are all there are.

But the history of music is much longer than a mere two hundred years. There was an awful lot of music sung and played *before* Bach, using all kind of *other* modes. In the music of our own century, when composers have gotten tired of being stuck with major and minor modes all the time, there has been a big revival of those old pre-Bach modes. That's why Debussy used them, and other modern composers, like Hindemith and Stravinsky, and almost all the young songwriters of today's exciting pop music scene.

The modes have provided them with a fresh sound, a relief from the old, overused major and minor. For instance, if the swinging opening of "Along Comes Mary" had been written in the usual, everyday minor mode, it would sound like this:

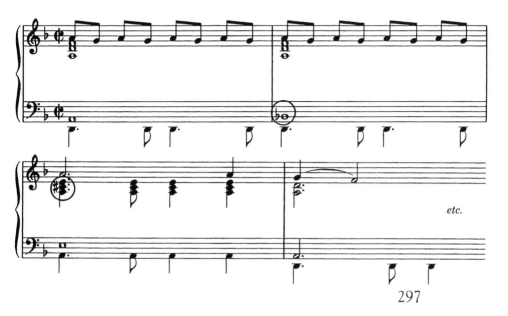

etc.

Sort of square, isn't it? Ordinary. But the real tune has a kick in it, and that kick is Dorian.

You can see that this Dorian mode is *almost* like an ordinary minor mode, but not quite. That *not quite* makes a big difference, one that gives the music a certain ancient, primitive, almost Oriental feeling. Thay's why the plainsong we heard before is so stirring, so ancient as to seem timeless. That's also why the tune in Debussy's *Fêtes* seems so exotic, and of another age; and it's why "Along Comes Mary" sounds so primitive and earthy.

By way of contrast, listen to this opening section of Sibelius's *Sixth Symphony*, which is also in the Dorian mode, and see if you can feel again that same timeless, brooding, ancient, far-off quality, only this time coming from the remote, lonely forests of Finland. (See the chapter on Sibelius, starting on p. 245.)

Are you beginning to feel the sound of the Dorian mode? Let's get technical for a minute, and find out just what it is that gives us this feeling. As we've learned, this Dorian mode is practically like our usual minor mode—with one very big difference, and that's on the seventh note of the scale:

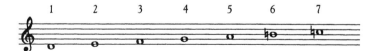

In the minor mode the seventh note—C-sharp (not C-natural)—is called the "leading tone" because it is supposed to lead us home to the keynote, or tonic note, which in this case, is D:

And that leading tone leads us to the tonic by the smallest interval possible, a half-tone:

It's as though that leading tone were in love with the tonic and were pulled toward it. It wants to embrace it, wants to get there, which it does. But in the Dorian mode, where the seventh note is a half-tone lower, there's a full whole tone between it and the tonic:

It just doesn't seem to lead as strongly. It's *not* in love with the tonic. It's friendly enough, but it just wants to shake hands. Do you feel how formal and *modal* that sounds? The minute we hear *that* "Amen," we feel behind it the weight of many centuries, of a different, older, more Eastern culture. Bach never wrote an "Amen" like that. Neither did Beethoven or Brahms. But in our own century it gets written all the time. For example, the Lennon-McCartney classic "Eleanor Rigby."

E - lea - nor Rig - by, picks up the rice ___ in the church ___ where a wed - ding has been ___ *etc.*

That's an awful lot about the Dorian mode—which, may you never forget as long as you live, starts on D. Dorian—D.

Let's get on to the next mode—which starts on E— the Phrygian mode. Again, this is also easy to find on the piano. You start on E, again play only white notes up to the next E, and there's your Phrygian mode:

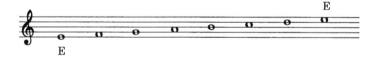

This Phrygian mode is very much like the Dorian in that it has a minor third step, and that lowered seventh step or leading tone:

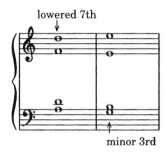

Another formal, strange mode. But it also has something very unusual: it is the only mode that *begins* with a step of a half-tone. From the first note, E, to the second note, F, is a mere half-step. This gives the music an especially sad quality, which can be heard in so much Spanish and Hebrew and Gypsy music. For instance, here's the beginning of Liszt's *Second Hungarian Rhapsody*, with its typical sad, Gypsy sound:

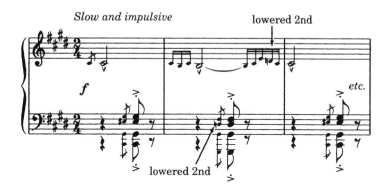

That's the Phrygian mode, a very Oriental-sounding one. But it has been much used by Western composers even during that famous two-hundred-year non-modal period, especially when they wanted to create Oriental effects. Take this well-known spot in the third movement of Rimsky-Korsakoff's *Scheherazade*, wildly Oriental:

301

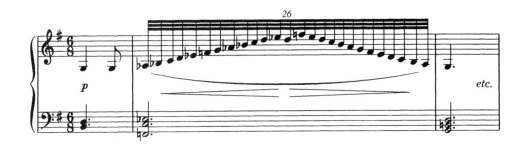

That's as about Oriental as you can get; and it's pure Phrygian:

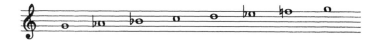

But the real surprise is to find even the old, very un-Oriental Johannes Brahms from Germany has used this mode—very unusual for him—in the slow movement of his *Fourth Symphony*. It begins with this solemn and majestic phrase:

The Phrygian mode, courtesy of Mr. Brahms.

Up we climb to the next mode, which is called Lydian. This one, logically, begins on F, and like the others, uses only white notes all the way up the octave:

What makes this Lydian mode different from the other minor-sounding modes we've discussed? Here's a normal F-major scale:

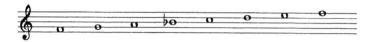

Lydian is also a major-sounding mode, the first one we've met so far; but its scale has a peculiar note. Can you figure out which note that is?

Bingo!, if you picked the fourth note of the scale, which is a half-tone higher than the so-called "normal" one. That's what gives this mode a very funny quality, almost comical, as if a wrong note were being played on purpose. In fact, many twentieth-century composers have taken advantage of this Lydian mode to get comic effects. For instance, Prokofieff, in his music for the funny film *Lieutenant Kije,* used this mode, with the raised fourth tone in the very opening, a piccolo solo:

If this had been written in the straight major scale, it would have sounded like this:

But no: Prokofieff adds his comic touch by using that Lydian raised fourth note.[6]

But I don't want you to think that the Lydian mode is only comical. On the contrary, it can be a very serious mode indeed. In fact, Beethoven wrote a whole long, serious movement of a string quartet in this very mode;[7] and, of course, it's still used in Roman Catholic plainsong in church. And again, Sibelius, who was always a great lover of modes, constantly used the Lydian mode, as in this passage from his *Fourth Symphony*:

The Lydian note in this instance is not a funny note, but a strange, piercing one that seems to come from a faraway place. That's only natural, because these modes do come from far away—like the Middle East and Eastern

European countries like Greece, Bulgaria, Finland, Russia, and Poland. In fact, Poland is one of the main breeding grounds for this Lydian mode. You constantly hear it in the works of Poland's greatest composer, who was Frédéric Chopin, especially when he was writing Polish-type dance pieces, like polonaises and mazurkas. Here's a bit from one of his best-known mazurkas. This time I won't point to the Lydian note. See if you can identify it yourself:

Lydian is an odd sound, so fresh and sharp, like the taste of lemon juice. And it's a very *Polish* sound. In fact, when the Russian composer Moussorgsky was writing the Third Act of his great opera *Boris Godunov*, an act which takes place in *Poland,* he used this same tangy Polish mode for his *Polonaise,* which means "Polish dance":[8]

So far we have had a good look at three important modes: Dorian, Phrygian, and Lydian—those white-note scales that start on D, E, and F, respectively. Here's a quick look at the remaining ones, starting with the mode that begins on G and rises up through the octave on the white notes. This one is called—don't panic!—the Mixolydian mode. Despite its tongue-twisting name, it's one of the most appealing and popular modes of all. Again, like its neighbor, the Lydian, it's a major-sounding mode, and also like the Lydian, it has one peculiar note in it, only this time it's a different peculiar note. Here's a normal G-major scale:

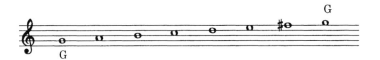

Here's the Mixolydian scale:

Lo and behold, it turns out that the seventh note, the leading tone we talked about before, is a half-tone lower than normal. This is the only major-sounding mode that has a lowered leading tone. What's more, believe it or not, most jazz and Afro-Cuban music and rock 'n' roll owe their very existence to this old Mixolydian mode. I could give you endless examples, but just to take one smash hit—*Hanky-Panky* by Jeff Barry and Ellie Greenwich:

That's Mixolydian. Or do you remember a really terrific song of a few years ago, sung by The Kinks?

Girl,   you real‑ly   got me go‑ing,   you got me

so I don't know what I'm do‑ing, __   *etc.*

Also pure Mixolydian. Or take the charming Beatles tune called "Norwegian Wood":

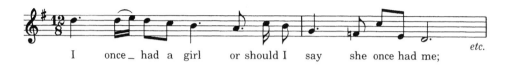

I   once __ had a girl   or should I   say   she once had me;   *etc.*

Again, with that lowered seventh note, it's Mixolydian gold.

Just as the Lydian mode did not just produce comic effects, I don't want to give you the idea that the Mixolydian mode produces only jazz or pop music. It's still to be heard in churches as well as in discotheques. In fact, our friend Debussy, in his piano prelude called *The Sunken Cathedral,* used the Mixolydian, an impressive cathederal‑like sonority:

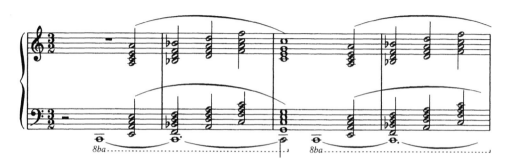

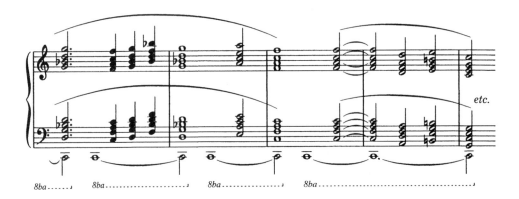

Years ago, when I was writing my first ballet, *Fancy Free,* I also used Mixolydian for one of the dances. Since it was a Cuban-style dance called a *danzón,* I naturally used this mode from beginning to end. Here's a bit of it:

In the few minutes that remain to us, I would like to pay my brief respects to the three modes we still haven't discussed. We can do this very quickly because the first

308

one, known as the Aeolian mode (which luckily starts on A, making it easy to remember), is almost like our "normal" minor scale. Using all the white notes, it is, in fact, sometimes referred to as the "natural minor" mode. Its one special feature is, again, that lowered leading tone which makes it so similar to the Dorian and Phrygian modes that we don't even have to discuss it any further. So "amen" to that:

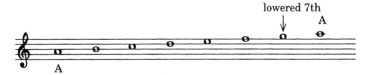

The sixth mode, starting on B, is known as the Locrian:

This one we can really skip, because there is almost no music written in it because the Locrian mode is strangely unsatisfying. It's inconclusive mainly due to the chord built on the tonic note, which is so unsettled and unresolved:

See what I mean? So hello and goodbye to the Locrian mode.

Now that we have been through the white-note modes, starting on D and going straight up the scale through E, F, G, A, and B, we at last come to C. Up we go, white notes only, to the next C:

What have we got? Surprise: the C-major scale! Good old, tried and true C-major of Bach, Beethoven, Brahms, and company. Once known as the Ionian, the C-major mode has survived, better than all its neighbors, and has emerged in glory as king of all Western music for two hundred years. For instance, a tremendous C-major moment by Beethoven celebrates this king of all modes. I'm talking about the final minute—the Coda—of the greatest movement in C-major ever built: Beethoven's *Fifth Symphony*. Here, at last, you won't have to worry about raised fourth-steps and lowered leading tones. For the time being, you can say goodbye to Beatles, Kinks, even Debussy, and just drink up the majesty and strength of this triumphant C-major festival by Beethoven. No doubt about it. It's C-major with a vengeance as Beethoven hammers it home:

Well, by now you've read enough about modes, and looked at enough examples of them, so that I think you're ready to turn to Debussy's *Fêtes* again, and this time really connect with it. To refresh your memory, recall the opening dance tune in the *Dorian* mode:

Then, a little later on, the switch to the *Lydian* mode, the Polish one with the raised fourth note:

311

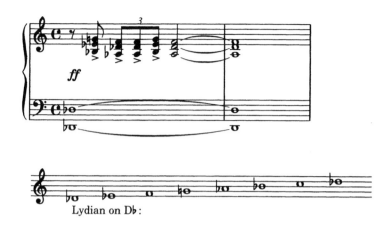

Lydian on D♭:

Then, a few seconds later, he's suddenly in the Mixo-lydian mode, the jazzy one with the lowered leading tone:

Mixolydian on A:

In the first half-minute of the piece, Debussy has used three different modes: Dorian, Lydian, and Mixolydian, no major or minor. In the middle section, when the distant procession begins, we're back first again in the Dorian:

The end of that example is in Phrygian, but it immediately switches to Mixolydian:

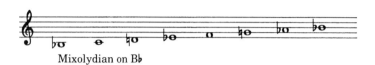

Mixolydian on B♭

So on it goes, one mode after the other, throughout the whole piece. But there is one particularly thrilling spot, a wonderful moment when the procession music and the dance music come crashing together. The trick is that they're both in the Dorian mode, making them perfect mates. This is the dance music:

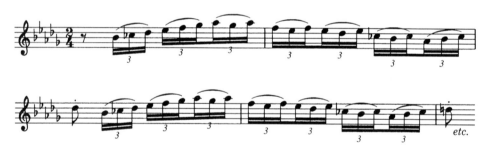

This the march music:

314

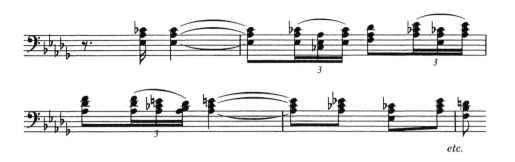

etc.

—and here are the two of them together:

etc.

It's a staggering sound. Listen to the entire piece. I hope you will hear it with new ears. You ought to, you know, since you are now Masters of Modes. So if people ask you what modes are, as my daughter asked me, you can give them a nice long lecture.

315

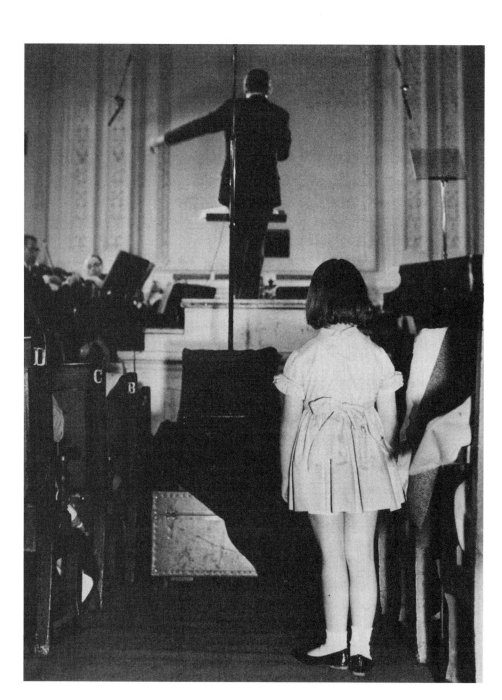

$\mathscr{B}$erlioz Takes a Trip

Pretty spooky stuff can be heard in the first psychedelic symphony in history. This first musical description of a "trip" was written one hundred thirty-odd years before the Beatles, way back in 1830 by the brilliant French composer Hector Berlioz. (That's Berlioz: the z is pronounced.) He called it *Symphonie Fantastique,* or "Fantastic Symphony," and fantastic it is, in every sense of the word, including psychedelic. That's not just my own idea about it. It's a fact because Berlioz himself tells us so. Just read the first two sentences of his own program note that he wrote describing the symphony:

> *A young musician of a morbidly sensitive nature and a feverish imagination poisons himself with opium in a fit of lovesick despair. The narcotic dose, too weak to cause death, plunges him into a heavy sleep accompanied by the strangest visions, during which his feelings, sensations and memories are translated by his sick brain into musical thoughts and images.*

Doesn't sound very different from these days, does it? And we have every reason to suspect that the morbid young musician Berlioz is talking about is none other than Hector himself. Because he certainly had fits of lovesick despair, we're told,[1] and he was a creature of wild imagination—wild enough to have these visions and fantasies without taking a dose of anything. His opium was simply his genius, which could transform these grotesque fantasies into music. Now read the next sentence of his program note:

> *Even the beloved one herself has become for him a melody, like a fixed idea which he hears everywhere, always returning.*

A *fixed idea*—or in French *une idée fixe*—in other words, an obsession. You all know what an obsession is: something that takes hold of your mind and won't let go. Well, in this symphony the obsession is Berlioz's beloved, she who has made him so desperately lovesick. She haunts the symphony; wherever the music goes, she keeps intruding, interrupting, returning in endless forms and shapes.

So you can see that if we're going to understand anything about this weird symphony, the first thing we have to know is the *idée fixe* melody, the theme of the beloved, and be able to recognize it each time it appears, no matter how it's disguised. Here it is, or at least the first phrase of it as played by the flute alone:

Can you hear the yearning in that melody? The way it has a rising shape at the beginning?

—then rising even higher, straining still further:

—then even further:

—then hopelessly collapsing:

etc.

Isn't that a perfect musical picture of lovesick longing? Look at it again, this time letting it continue into its second phrase, then its third, fourth, and so on, each time rising and straining further, and each time again falling back into despair:

320

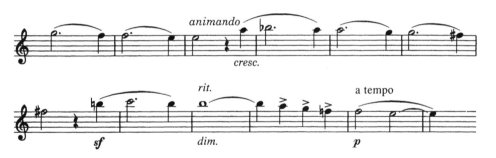

I'm sure that any of you who has ever had a crush on someone who didn't return your feelings will understand that passionate melody perfectly; and you can easily see how a lovesick musician could become obsessed by it. If you understand that, you're ready to hear the symphony.

The first movement is subtitled "Visions and Passions." It begins with a slow, dreamlike introduction, which we're going to skip since it only prepares the atmosphere for the entrance of the main theme. In other words, it paints for us the dreamy, romantic lover *before* the obsession hits him. But when it *does* hit—oh boy!, just listen. Here's the end of the introduction as it leads into the first feverish outburst of the *idée fixe* theme—and watch for those psychedelic fireworks:

Do you get what I meant by "psychedelic fireworks"? Those sudden flashes and changes of color, the dazzling unexpectedness of those dynamic changes—the changes from loud to soft and back again. There are dozens of them! Just look: in those few opening bars before the main theme comes in there are all these dynamic changes

in rapid succession: mezzo-forte—diminuendo—pianissimo—crescendo—fortissimo—sudden triple piano!—
sudden fortissimo—sudden piano—pianissimo—fortissimo—piano—pianissimo—mezzo-forte—triple pianissimo— What a preparation, what a display of fireworks,
of mind-flashes, of romantic fever? And then when the
theme does come in, each of those rising and surging
phrases is written with its own little burstof crescendo:

And notice how Berlioz accompanies his melody. Very
strangely indeed: with no accompaniment at all *under*
the melody, but *between* the phrases there are jerky little
figures in the strings:

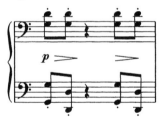

They're so uneven, always popping in where you don't
expect them. Then the way the *tempo* is always changing,
charging breathlessly ahead, then slowing up, then suddenly in time again, suddenly slowing up again. You
never know what's coming: flash-changes, changes of
dynamics, of tempo, of color, and all of it resting pre-
cariously on that crazy, jerky accompaniment. I tell you,
you can become a nervous wreck playing this symphony.
But then, that's what it is: a portrait of a nervous wreck.

By now, then, you ought to have that theme down
pat, so that you can follow it in all its grotesque, psy-

chedelic disguises and developments: through anxiety, jealousy, rage, and despair—the works. The rest of this first movement is almost all such developments of the theme. We can't go over all of them, but let's have a couple, just to see how they work. Here's one, where the low strings take up the theme, in a growling, menacing way, while over them the woodwinds and horns are heaving a series of heartbreaking sighs. This is a perfect picture of the agony of jealous rage:

Did you see how that works up into a climax of anguish? But if you think *that* is anguished, listen to how it goes on, with the sighs growing into *howls* and the strings rising to hysterical shrieks:

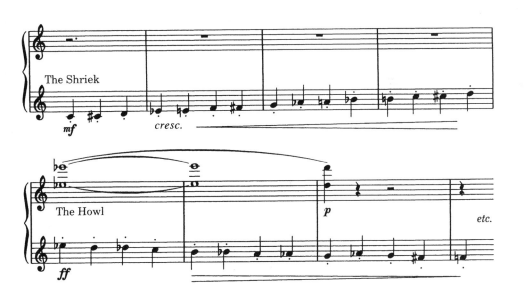

Twelve bars later, the howling and shrieking get even more intense; he almost flips his lid:

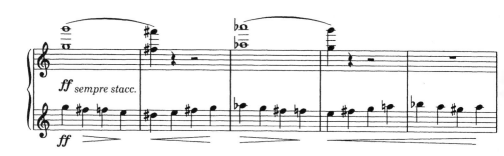

This music sometimes comes dangerously close to the borderline of sanity. Every once in a while you think it may just go over the line, but it never does. Berlioz is always in control, no matter how insane he seems to get. That's genius.

Just one more passage in this first movement, the weirdest of all. This time the low strings are again moaning away on the *idée fixe* tune, only now in canon[2] with the violas imitating the cellos like a bunch of lovesick cattle. Here first are the cellos moaning:

You certainly know that tune. And here are the violas imitating them:

Here's how they come together, in canon:

But all that is only the groundwork. Above that rises a new melody in the oboe, having nothing to do with the main theme—in fact, having nothing to do with *anything* much except maybe modern music, music to be written a century later. This long melodic line is one of those musical monuments in history, unlike anything else of its time, so weird that you can almost not tell what key it's in or indeed if it's in a key at all. It's a marvelous representation of a sick, wandering mind, a desperate soul; but the mind that composed it was anything but sick. It was pure genius. The mad oboe begins:

Wow! Can you believe that was written in 1830, only three years after the death of classical old Beethoven? It sounds more like *1930*, as though it were by Hindemith or Shostakovich or somebody like that. On and on that oboe goes, rising dizzily over the canon of those moaning

328

strings, soaring to a new climax of hallucination. When it gets there, the whole orchestra joins in, including trumpets for the first time, with the *idée fixe* melody in full swing of triumph, as though Berlioz had at last conquered his mania. But no, the madness takes hold again, dynamic flashes and all, and suddenly everything falls apart. The music splinters, like a smashed window, and finally dies away out of sheer exhaustion. In the final bars we hear one last longing whisper of the *idée fixe* melody, and the movement ends with a few organ-like chords of religious comfort.

End of Scene I, and end of dream one. Now a new dream; new scenery: an elegant ballroom, at first shadowy, gradually becoming lighter and brighter, until we are in the midst of a brilliant party. Two harps now join the orchestra, giving a ringing shine to the music, which is, of course, a waltz, a charming, whirling French waltz. But after a minute or so the tune changes mysteriously— to what? Guess! To the *idée fixe*, naturally, and there, indeed, is the beloved's face appearing and vanishing among the dancers. The desperate lover reaches out for her, but she is never there. The more he reaches, the more she eludes him. The waltz goes on, and finally hits its climax—and suddenly everything stops. Nothing is there but *the* tune, the obsession, and for a moment it seems possible that he will have her, hold her. But then the waltz-world crashes in on him, he is separated from her by all those thousands of waltzers, whirling faster and faster around him, and he wakes up. Another fantastic nightmare.

One of the most fantastic things about this *Fantastic Symphony* is when it was written. Berlioz is exactly one century dead this year [1969], which is a staggering fact, considering how modern his music sounds; but it's even more staggering to realize that when he died, this symphony of his was already almost half a century old. Just think of it, this wild music was written way back in 1830, as I said before, just three years after old Beethoven had died; and Berlioz was only a lad of twenty-six when he wrote this incredible new music. I mean *new*: just try to think how amazing this *Fantastique* must have sounded in 1830, even after the wildest late works of Beethoven. This youthful symphony must have seemed to come from a whole other planet, a new world called Romanticism.

For instance, take this third movement coming up, a "Scene in the Countryside." Beethoven had already written *his* scene in the countryside, the famous *Pastoral Symphony*, with its shepherd calls, bird calls, murmuring brooks, and raging storms. But they were nothing compared to this Berlioz movement. He writes real thunder, using four different timpani players, something old Beethoven would never have thought of. And Berlioz's shepherds don't just play their pipes, they play out a whole drama.

The idea of the drama in this movement is that our poor drugged lover is now dreaming a scene in the country. For a moment it's not a nightmare anymore, but a peaceful dream of nature's beauty and repose. There's a shepherd playing to his flocks, who's answered by another shepherd way off on a distant slope. This duet of the shepherds at the beginning is somehow comforting to our hero's loneliness. There *is* human communication in the world, even if people are far away from each other. Let's eavesdrop, just for a moment, on those two shepherds:

That's a romantic piece of tone-painting: you can almost see the alpine country scene. Into this atmosphere Berlioz's hero dreams peacefully for a long while; the birds call sweetly, there seems to be hope in his life. We'll skip that part (it's all too hopeful). But suddenly the atmosphere changes, the skies darken, agitation seizes the music, and Guess Who appears, taunting him with the *idée fixe* melody, a wolf-girl in sheep's clothing. Here is that moment of truth:

331

What a nightmare. What a marvelous picture of panic
and terror, with that breathless panting as it gradually
subsides. Again there is some kind of peace and quiet.
Our dreamer seems to be saved again from his obsession;
but Berlioz has another horror up his sleeve, the final
page of the movement. In this one extraordinary page
he gives us a dramatic picture of the pain of loneliness
that has never been equaled, not even by the most neu-
rotic composers of our own century. What happens is
this: the shepherd begins this tune again, one phrase.
We wait for the answer from his distant friend, but there
is no answer. Instead, only a mysterious rumble of thunder. The shepherd tries again, another phrase; again the
hollow answer of thunder:

Little by little the scene fades. The shepherd gives up
completely, the thunder dies away completely, and our
dreamer is left alone with the terrifying silence of love-
lessness.

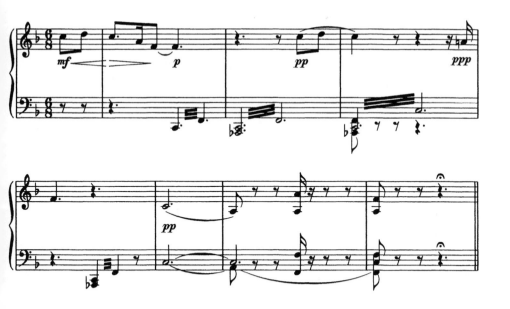

Scene four, or fourth movement. Change of scene: a new nightmare. In this dream he is a murderer, and whom has he murdered? Guess. His beloved, naturally; and the scene is the place of execution. He must now pay for his crime at the guillotine. This whole movement is a gruesome march, complete with the drums and brass of the execution squad. A great march, brilliant and horrible at the same time. Finally our agonized dreamer arrives at the scaffold, and bows his head to the blade. The music is by now savage, out of its mind, when suddenly, as happens in dreams, everything stops; and for one instant he sees (or hears?) his beloved: the *idée fixe, that* melody. But only for an instant. The familiar phrase hangs there in the air, and bang!, it's cut off along with our hero's head. A roll of drums, a blare of brass, end of nightmare. Here's how his head gets chopped off in the fourth movement:

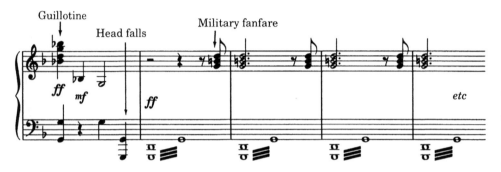

Wait, it's not over yet! There's a fifth and final dream that even tops that one: the "Nightmare of the Witches' Sabbath," which is the topper of the whole trip. The lover now is dreaming he is dead; he is at his own funeral. But this is no solemn funeral. There are no holy words and no prayers. Only the grisly shrieks of witches:

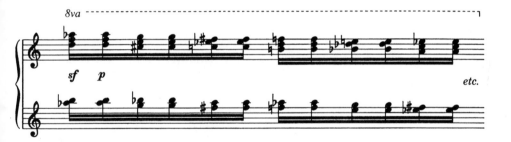

—and the bloodcurdling laughter of demons and devils:

—and the diabolical dancing of Halloween hags and grinning monsters:

335

And, of course, who should be the chief witch? None other than that sweet little beloved of his, whose angelic melody is now transformed into a hellish, squealing ride on a broomstick:

Then there are spine-chilling funeral bells:

—and a parody of the *Dies Irae*, the chant from the [Catholic] Mass for the Dead:

And much, much more—but I want to leave something for your own imagination.

All this horror builds up into a most brilliant ending, but brilliant or not, I'm sorry to say it leaves our hero still in the clutches of his opium nightmare. It's brilliance without glory—that's the problem. I can't honestly tell you that we have gone through the fires of hell with our hero and come out the better for it, nobler and wiser. But that's the way with trips, and Berlioz tells it like it is. Now *there* was an honest man.

You take a trip, you wind up screaming at your own funeral. Take a tip from Berlioz: that music is all you need for the wildest trip you can take, to hell and back. With drugs you might make it, but you might not make it back.

Notes

1. They included Aaron Copland, Dean Dixon, Yehudi Menuhin, Peter Ustinov, and Michael Tilson Thomas.

2. Two of Englander's assistants, acknowledged by Leonard Bernstein in his Foreword, have gone one to achieve wider recognition in the music field: Mary Rodgers, as a musical theater writer; and John Corigliano, as one of the leading American composers of the current generation.

Chapter One

1. Musicians call this "spiccato."

2. The background score for the film 2001: A Space Odyssey uses this Strauss piece.

339

Chapter Two

1. *Translation: "In a field a little birch tree stands; in a field a curly-headed tree. . ."*

2. Of course, 1976 marked the bicentennial year of the United States.

3. This Largo movement tune by Dvořák was set to words by William Arms Fisher as "Goin' Home." Thought by many to be an authentic spiritual, it is "actually a white man's text to a white European's music" (Great Symphonies by Sigmund Spaeth).

Chapter Three

1. Some of these "anonymous" orchestrations include those who scored Bernstein Broadway shows: Hershey Kay, Don Walker, Sid Ramin, and Irwin Kostal.

2. The technical term for this phenomenon is synesthesia.

3. See page 12 for a description of the effects produced by violins playing "spiccato."

Chapter Four

1. As it turns out, Mr. Bernstein's hair turned completely white.

Chapter Five

1. Or Michael Jackson, or name your favorite pop star.

2. *There are many references to Beethoven's Fifth Symphony throughout the book. See pages 76, 78–80, 105–6, 183, 202, 205, 207, 310–11.*

3. *Strictly speaking, the first half of the eighteenth century is considered the Baroque, or pre-Classical, period.*

4. *For a fuller discussion of intervals, see Chapter Thirteen.*

5. *In fact, this structure is so well built by Bach that the theme of the fugue never appears* alone, *even at the very beginning, but is always heard along with a supporting counter-theme, just as a beam in any building is supported by a pillar. In this case, the viola entrance is supported by the bass and harpsichord.*

6. *In this connection, you might want to listen to the scherzo from Beethoven's Symphony No. 7.*

7. *Similarly, Mahler has been characterized as the last man of the Romantic period, and one of the first of the so-called modern period.*

Chapter Six

1. *Composer John Cage, who includes chance-sounds in his definition of what constitutes music, would not agree.*

Chapter Seven

1. *The magazine was McCall's.*

2. *In fact, Vivaldi wrote more than five hundred concertos.*

3. *It was called the Ospedale della Pietà, a Venetian institution for illegitimate or orphaned girls.*

4. *The title is a mouthful:* Concerto in Do Maggiore per due flauti, due tiorbe, due mandolini, due salmoè, due violini in tromba marina e violoncello, *Op. 64 (Cat. R.), No. 6.*

5. The salmo is known in English as the shawm.

6. Note that Vivaldi also wrote concertos for solo instrument and orchestra, the most famous of them being Le quattro stagione, Op. 8, or The Four Seasons, a set of four concertos for solo violin and orchestra.

7. Heifetz, Cliburn and Casals, virtuosos on violin, piano and cello, respectively.

Chapter Eight

1. Translation: "Come home, dear mother."

2. Translation: "There was a little boat, that never sailed . . ."

3. All the notes, that is, except B-flat.

Chapter Nine

1. That is, as of 1961, the date of this Young People's Concert.

Chapter Eleven

1. Mr. Bernstein discussed this earlier. See p. 153.

2. Now called Avery Fisher Hall, at Lincoln Center, New York City.

3. Soprano Veronica Tyler sang Micaela's aria Je dis, que rien ne m'épouvante ("I say that I am not afraid") from Carmen with the orchestra. Translation: "I say that I am

not afraid, I say, alas, that I speak for myself, but there is no point in being brave . . . I'll be face to face with that woman, whose cursed air turned a man into an outlaw . . . I say that I am not afraid . . ."

4. One of the most frustrating things a beginning student in music theory learns is "you have to know the rules before you can break them."

Chapter Thirteen

1. It is also called "retrograde" motion

2. The process is known, therefore, as "inversion."

3. Brahms's Fourth Symphony is also mentioned on pages 149, 269—73, 285, and 302.

Chapter Fourteen

1. The word scale comes from Latin scala, meaning "ladder." La Scala is the name of the opera house in Milan, Italy.

2. Other differences concern the whole- and half-step arrangements of the sixth and seventh steps of the scale, which provide us with the natural or so-called melodic and harmonic-minor scales.

3. You will recall the word Doric, one of the three orders of Greek architecture.

4. In fact, most of the modes are named after Grecian territorial locations: the confederacies of Dorian, Ionian, and Aeolian cities, as well as the Lydian and Phrygian territories.

5. "Along Comes Mary" by Tandyn Almer was one of the big hits for the '60s group called The Association.

343

6. In the original draft for this program, Mr. Bernstein also mentioned: "And our own American composer, Aaron Copland, used the same device in his music for a comic scene in the film Of Mice and Men." After citing an example, he said: "There's that funny note again." It should be noted, also, that Copland used the Lydian mode for a very beautiful, non-funny aria: "Queenie's song" in his school opera The Second Hurricane, heard in Young People's Concert No. 11. It was performed by Julia Migenes, who grew up to be a world-renowned opera star.

7. In the Beethoven String Quartet in A-minor, Op. 132, the Adagio movement is subtitled: "Song of Thanksgiving to God from a Convalescent, in the Lydian Mode."

8. The word polonaise, however, comes from French, meaning "Polish."

Chapter Fifteen

1. Apparently Berlioz received the love-bite from an Irish actress named Harriet Smithson. Even though he did not understand a word of English, he was smitten by her after seeing, in Paris, her portrayals of Shakespearean heroines.

2. See p. 88 for a definition of canon.

Chronological List
of Young People's Concerts
Written and Performed
by Leonard Bernstein
with the New York Philharmonic

Original Air Dates

1. What Does Music Mean?   January 18, 1958

EXCERPTS FROM:*

William Tell Overture	Rossini
Don Quixote	Strauss
Symphony No. 6	Beethoven
Pictures at an Exhibition	Moussorgsky
Symphonies Nos. 4 and 5	Tchaikovsky
Six Pieces	Webern
La Valse (complete)	Ravel

2. What Is American Music?   February 1, 1958

EXCERPTS FROM:

An American in Paris	Gershwin
Symphony No. 5	Dvořák
Dance in Place Congo	Gilbert
Ragtime	Stravinsky
Rhapsody in Blue	Gershwin
American Festival Overture	Schuman
Symphony No. 3	Harris
Symphony No. 2	Thompson
The Mother of Us All	Thomson

*Note: Brief examples, less than thirty seconds long and usually played on piano, are not given

Music for the Theatre . . . . Copland
Billy the Kid . . . . Copland
Symphony No. 3 . . . . .Copland, conducted by
the composer

3. What Is Orchestration? March 8, 1958

EXCERPTS FROM:

Capriccio Espagnol . . . . . .Rimsky-Korsakoff
Brandenburg Concerto No. 3 . . . . . . Bach
Kleine Kammermusik
for Wind Quintet . . . . Hindemith
Serenade in B-flat, No. 10, K. 361 . . . . Mozart
Fantasia on a Theme
by Thomas Tallis . . . . . .Vaughn Williams
Symphony for Strings . . . . Schuman
Introduction and Allegro . . . . . .Ravel
L'Histoire du Soldat . . . . Stravinsky
Bolero (complete) . . . . . . .Ravel

4. What Makes Music
Symphonic? December 13, 1958

EXCERPTS FROM:

Symphony No. 4 . . . . . . Tchaikovsky
Symphony No. 3, "Eroica" . . . . . . Beethoven
Overture Fantasy:
Romeo and Juliet . . . . . . Tchaikovsky
Symphony No. 104, "London" . . . . . Haydn
Symphony No. 41, "Jupiter" . . . . . Mozart
Symphony No. 2 . . . . Brahms

5. What Is Classical Music? January 24, 1959

EXCERPTS FROM:

Symphony No. 102 in B-Flat . . . . . Haydn
Symphony No. 40 in G-minor . . . . . Mozart
Overture: The Marriage of Figaro . . . . . Mozart
Concerto No. 21 in C-Major, K. 467 . . . . Mozart
Overture: Egmont (complete) . . . . . . Beethoven

6. Humor in Music   February 28, 1959

EXCERPTS FROM:

Symphony No. 88, Finále   .   .   .   .   .   .   Haydn
Classical Symphony,. Myts. I and II   .   .   .   .   Prokofieff
Symphony No. 1, segment of Mvt. II   .   .   .   .   Mahler
"Polka" from The Golden Age   .   .   .   .   Shostakovich
"Burlesque" from Music
   for the Theatre   .   .   .   .   Copland
Symphony No. 4, Scherzo .   .   .   .   .   .   Brahms

ALSO EXCERPTS FROM WORKS BY:

Piston, Paul White, Gershwin, Mozart, Kodály,
   Wagner, and Richard Strauss

7. What Is a Concerto?   March 28, 1959

EXCERPTS FROM:

Concerto for Two Mandolins, Strings,
   and Cembalo, Mvt. I   .   .   .   .   .   .   Vivaldi
Brandenburg Concerto No. 5 in D-Major, for
   Harpsichord, Violin, Flute, and Strings,
   Finale .   .   .   . Bach
(John Corigliano, Sr., violin; John Wummer, flute;
   John Bernstein, harpsichord, soloists)
Sinfonia Concertante for Violin, Viola, and Orchestra
   in E-Flat Major, K. 364, Mvt. II   .   .   .   .   Mozart
Concerto for Violin and Orchestra in E-Minor,
   Finale .   .   .   .   Mendelssohn
(John Corigliano, Sr., soloist)
Concerto for Orchestra, Mvts. V and VI   .   .   .   Bartók

8. Who Is Gustav Mahler?   February 7, 1960

EXCERPTS FROM:

Symphonies Nos. 4, 2, and 1
Das Lied von der Erde
Des Knaben Wunderhorn
(Reri Grist, soprano; Helen Raab, contralto; William
   Lewis, tenor, soloists)

347

9. Young Performers No. 1   March 6, 1960

EXCERPTS FROM:

Concerto for Cello and Orchestra in B-Minor,
Mvt I . . . . Dvořák
(Daniel Domb, age 15, cello; Kenneth Schermerhorn,
   conductor)
Concerto for Violin and Orchestra No. 2,
Finale . . . . Wieniawski
(Barry Finclair, age 14, violin; Stefan B. Mengelberg,
   conductor)
Peter and the Wolf . . . . Prokofieff
Alexandra Wager, age 9, narrator; Leonard Bernstein, conductor)

10. Unusual Instruments of
    Present, Past, and Future   March 27, 1960

EXCERPTS FROM:

Toccata: "Little Train of Caipira" (from
   Bachianas Brasileiras No. 2) . . . . . Villa-Lobos
Brandenburg Concerto No. 4, Mvt. I . . . . . Bach
Canzon Septimi Toni . . . . Gabrielli
Alta, Spanish Dance (ca. 1500) . . . . . De LaTorre
(Members of New York Pro Musica, soloists; Noah Greenberg, Musical
   Director)
Concerted Piece for Tape Recorder and
   Orchestra . . . . Luening-Ussachevsky
(Vladimir Ussachevsky, tape recorder soloist)
Concerto for a Singing Instrument, Mvt. III:
   "Tug of War" . . . . Bucci
(Premiere; Anita Darian, kazoo soloist)

11. The Second Hurricane   April 24, 1960

PLAY-OPERA IN TWO ACTS:

Words by Edwin Denby; Music by Aaron Copland
(Cast from High School of Music and Art, New York City
Mrs. R. Sybil Mandel, Music Chairman
Soloists: Steven Wertheimer as Butch; Julian Liss as Fat; John
Richardson as Gyp; Lawrence Willis as Lowrie; Omega Milbourne
as Gwen; Marion Cowings as Jeff; Julie Makis as Queenie; Senior
Choral Ensemble)

12. Overtures and Preludes   January 8, 1961

    Overture: Semiramide .   .   .   .   Rossini
    Overture: Leonore   .   .   .   . Beethoven
    Prelude to the Afternoon of a Faun   .   .   .   . Debussy
    Overture: Candide   .   .   .   . Bernstein

13. Aaron Copland Birthday Party   February 12, 1961

    EXCERPTS FROM COPLAND WORKS

    Statements for Orchestra No. 3: "Dogmatic"
    Music for the Theatre No. 2: "Dance"
    Music for Movies No. 4: "Grover's Corners"
    Rodeo: "Hoedown"
    Old American Songs: "Boatman's Dance,"
    "I Bought Me a Cat" (William Warfield, baritone)
    El Salón México (Aaron Copland, conductor)

14. Young Performers No. 2   March 19, 1961

    EXCERPTS FROM:

    Concerto for Cello & Orchestra in B-Minor,
        Op. 104: Finale   .   .   .   .   Dvořák
    (Lynn Harrell, age 16, cello; Elyakum Shapira, conductor)
    Concerto No. 1 in E-Minor, Op. 11:
        Mvt. II   .   .   .   .   Chopin
    (Jung Ja Kim, age 16, piano; Russell Stanger, conductor)
    Aria: "Hello, Hello" from
        The Telephone   .   .   .   .   Menotti
    Aria: "Mimì's Farewell"
        from *La Bohème*   .   .   .   .   Puccini
    (Veronica Tyler, age 22, soprano; Gregory Millar, conductor)
    Young Person's Guide to the Orchestra   .   .   .   .   Britten
    (Henry Chapin, age 12, narrator; Leonard Bernstein, conductor)

15. Folk Music in the Concert Hall   April 9, 1961

    EXCERPTS FROM:

    Symphony No. 39 in E-Flat, K. 543, Minuet .   .   .   Mozart
    Sinfonía India .   .   .   .   Chávez
    Songs of the Auvergne.   .   .   .   arranged by Canteloube

349

(Marni Nixon, soprano soloist)
Symphony No. 2, Finale . . . . Ives

16. What Is Impressionism?   December 1, 1961

La Mer (complete) . . . . Debussy
Daphnis et Chloé, Suite No. 2, Finale . . . . . Ravel

17. The Road to Paris   January 18, 1962

EXCERPTS FROM:

An American in Paris . . . . Gershwin
Schelomo . . . . Bloch
(Zara Nelsova, cello soloist)
The Three-Cornered Hat: Two Dances . . . . De Falla

18. Happy Birthday, Igor Stravinsky   March 26, 1962

WORKS BY STRAVINSKY:

Greeting Prelude
Petrouchka (Ballet in 4 Scenes, complete)

19. Young Performers No. 3   April 14, 1962

Overture: The Marriage of Figaro . . . . . Mozart
(Seiji Ozawa, conductor)
Prayer . . . . Bloch-Antonini
(Gary Karr, double bass; Maurice Peress, conductor)
Fantasy on a Theme from the
   Opera Moses in Egypt . . . . Paganini-Reinshagen
(Gary Karr, double bass; John Canarina, conductor)
Carnival of the Animals . . . . . . Saint-Saëns
SOLOISTS:
   Ruth & Naomi Segal, age 21, duo-pianists
   Paula Robison, age 20, flute
   Paul Green, age 13, clarinet
   Tony Cirone, age 20, xylophone
   Gary Karr, age 20, double bass
   David Hopper, age 14, glockenspiel

20. The Sound of a Hall   November 21, 1962

Overture: Roman Carnival, Opus 9   .   .   .   .   Berlioz
"The Little Horses" from
   Old American Songs   .   .   .   .   .   .   Copland
(Shirley Verrett-Carter, soprano)
Concerto for Four Violins and String Orchestra
   in B-Minor, Op. 10, No. 3, Mvt. I   .   .   .   .   Vivaldi
(John Corigliano, Sr., Frank Gullino, Joseph Bernstein,
   William Dembinsky, soloists)

21. What Is a Melody?   December 21, 1962

Prelude to Tristan and Isolde.   .   .   .   .   .   Wagner
Symphony No. 40 in G-Minor, K. 550, Mvt. I   .   .   Mozart
Concert Music for Strings and Brass Op. 50   .   .   . Hindemith
Symphony No. 4 in E-Minor, op. 98:
   Finale .   .   .   .   Brahms

22. Young Performers No. 4   January 15, 1963

Concerto for Piano and Orchestra in
   A-Major, K. 488 .   .   .   .   Mozart
Mvt. I: Joan Weiner, age 14, piano; Yuri
   Krasnopolsky, conductor
Mvt. II: Claudia Hoca, age 12, piano; Zoltan
   Rozsnyai, conductor
Mvt. III: Pamela Paul, age 13, piano; Serge
   Fournier, conductor
Concerto No. 1 for Piano and
   Orchestra in E-Flat Major.   .   .   .   .   .   . Liszt
(André Watts, age 16, piano; Leonard Bernstein, conductor)

23. The Latin American Spirit   March 8, 1963

"Batuque," from the Suite
   Reisado Do Pastoreio   .   .   .   .   .   . Fernandez
Bachianas Brasileiras No. 5 .   .   .   .   .   . Villa-Lobos
(Netania Davrath, soprano)
Sensemaya   .   .   .   . Revueltas
Symphonic Dances from West Side Story:
   Mambo, *Cha-Cha, Meeting Scene, "Cool"*
   (Fugue), *Rumble,* and *Finale* .   .   .   .   . Bernstein
Danzón Cubano   .   .   .   . Copland

24. A Tribute to Teachers   November 29, 1963

Prelude to Khovanshchina .   .   .   .   .   Moussorgsky
Symphony No. 2, Scherzo .   .   .   .   .   . Thompson
Suite from *The Incredible Flutist* .   .   .   .   Piston
Academic Festival Overture, Op. 80   .   .   .   Brahms

25. Young Performers No. 5   December 23, 1963

Concerto for Harp and Orchestra in B-Flat Major,
    Op. 4, No. 6, Mvt. I   .   .   .   .   .   . Handel
(Heidi Lehwalder, age 14, harp; Leonard Bernstein,
    conductor)
Introduction and Allegro for Harp, Flute,
    Clarinet and Strings. .   .   .   .   .   . Ravel
(Heidi Lehwalder; Amos Eisenberg, age 24, flute; Weldon Berry, Jr.,
    age 16, clarinet; Claudio Abbado, conductor)
Concerto for Piano and Orchestra
    (Premiere) .   .   .   . Ran
(Shulamith Ran, age, 16, piano/composer; Pedro Calderon, conductor)
Rhapsody No. 1 for Cello and Orchestra .   .   .   Bartók
(Stephen E. Kates, cello; Zdenek Kosler, conductor)
William Tell Overture. .   .   .   .   .   . Rossini

26. The Genius of Paul Hindemith   February 23, 1964

ALL MUSIC BY HINDEMITH

String Quartet No. 3, Op. 22
Kleine Kammermusik for Wind Quintet
Symphony: Mathis der Mahler

27. Jazz in the Concert Hall   March 11, 1964

Journey into Jazz .   .   .   . Schuller
(Gunther Schuller, composer and conductor)
Concerto for Piano and Orchestra .   .   .   .   Copland
(Aaron Copland, piano)
Improvisations for Orchestra and
    Jazz Soloists .   .   .   .   Austin

352

28. What Is Sonata Form?   November 6, 1964

Jupiter Symphony, Mvt. I . . . . . . Mozart
Sonata in C-Major . . . . Mozart
(Mr. Bernstein at the piano)
Classical Symphony, Mvt. IV . . . . . Prokofieff
A Hard Day's Night . . . . . Lennon-McCartney
(vocal by Mr. Bernstein at the piano)
Micaela's Aria from *Carmen* . . . . . . Bizet
(Veronica Tyler, soprano)

29. Farewell to Nationalism   November 30, 1964

EXCERPTS FROM:

Russian Sailor's Dance from *The Red
   Poppy)*. . . . . Gliére
Hungarian Rhapsody No. 2 . . . . . . Liszt
Five Pieces for Orchestra (complete)
   Opus 10, No. 1 . . . . . . Webern
*Pieces for Prepared Piano and
   String Quartet* . . . . Cage
Composition for Twelve Instruments . . . . Babbitt
Incontri Fuer 24, Instrumente . . . . . Nono
*Sonata in G-Minor for Flute and
   Harpsichord* . . . . Bach
*Concerto No. 41 in G-Minor for Flute, Bassoon,
   Violin, and Bass* . . . . . . Vivaldi
Prelude to Die Meistersinger . . . . . Wagner
Mazurka in B-Flat . . . . . . Chopin
Aria: "Sempre Libera" from *La Traviata* . . . Verdi
Symphony No. 4 . . . . . . Tchaikovsky
Battle Hymn of the Republic. . . . . . Steffe
Yankee Doodle . . . . Traditional
Columbia, the Gem of the Ocean: Beckett, as used in:
Fourth of July (from *Holiday Symphony*). . . . Ives
(Seymour Lipkin, co-conductor)
Suite No. 1: The Three-Cornered Hat . . . De Falla
The Moldau (My Country) . . . . . Smetana

30. Young Performers No. 6   January 28, 1965

*Concerto for Piano and Orchestra No. 20
   in D-Minor, Mvt. I* . . . . . Mozart
(Patricia Michaelian, age 15, piano)

Concerto for Violin and Orchestra in E-Minor,
Opus 64 Mvt. I: .   .   .   .   .   .   Mendelssohn
(James Buswell, age 18, violin)
Ma Mère l'Oye (Mother Goose)
   Suite (complete)   .   .   .   . Ravel

31. A Tribute to Sibelius   February 19, 1965

ALL MUSIC BY SIBELIUS:

Finlandia
Concerto for Violin and Orchestra in D-Major Opus 47
(Sergiu Luca, age 20, violin)
Symphony No. 2, Opus 43

32. Musical Atoms:
    A Study of Intervals   November 29, 1965

Prelude to Act III: Lohengrin   .   .   .   .   .   Wagner
"The Blue Danube" .   .   .   .   Strauss
Symphony No. 4, Mvt. I   .   .   .   .   .   .   Brahms
Symphony No. 4, Finale   .   .   .   .   Vaughan Williams

33. The Sound of an Orchestra   December 14, 1965

Symphony No. 88, Largo   .   .   .   .   .   .   Haydn
Symphony No. 5, Mvt. III, opening   .   .   .   . Beethoven
Symphony No. 7   .   .   .   . Beethoven
Symphony No. 1   .   .   .   . Brahms
Ibéria, Mvt. II, Finale   .   .   .   .   .   . Debussy
L'Histoire du Soldat: "The Royal
   March"   .   .   .   . Stravinsky
An American in Paris .   .   .   . Gershwin
Partita in E Major   .   .   .   . Bach
Rodeo: "Hoedown"   .   .   .   . Copland

34. A Birthday Tribute
    to Shostakovich   January 5, 1966

Symphony No. 7, Mvt. I .   .   .   .   .   Shostakovich
Symphony No. 9 (complete)   .   .   .   .   Shostakovich
Symphony No. 9, Finale (excerpt)   .   .   .   . Beethoven

35. Young Performers No. 7:
    Pictures at an Exhibition   February 22, 1966

Pictures at an Exhibition (original
    piano) . . . . Moussorgsky
"Promenade," "Gnomes" (Paul Schoenfeld, age 19, piano)
"Promenade," "The Old Castle" (Paul Schoenfield, age 19, piano)
"Promenade," "Tuileries," "Promenade," "Ballet of Chicks in Their
    Shells" (David Oei, age 15 piano)
"The Great Gate at Kiev" (Horacio Gutierrez, age 17, piano)

The above selections were followed by their orchestral transcriptions
by Ravel, conducted respectively by:
    James De Priest
    Jacques Houtmann
    Edo de Waart
    Leonard Bernstein

36. What Is a Mode?   November 23, 1966

Nocturnes: Fêtes . . . . Debussy
Boris Godunov: "Polonaise"
    from Act III . . . . Moussorgsky
Fancy Free: "Danzón" . . . . . . Bernstein
Fêtes repeated

37. Young Performers No. 8   January 27, 1967

Sinfonia Concertante . . . . Haydn
(Elmar Oliveira, age 16, violin; Mark Salkind, age 13, oboe; Fred
    Alston, age 19, bassoon; Donald Green, age 20, cello; Juan Pablo
    Izquierdo conducted
    Mvt. I; Sylvia Caduff conducted Mvts. II & III)
Concerto No. 2 for Piano
    and Orchestra in F-Minor, Finale . . . . Chopin
(transcribed for accordion and played by Stephen Dominko, age 19;
    Sylvia Caduff, conductor)
"In diesen heil'gen Hallen,"
    aria from *The Magic Flute* . . . . . Mozart
(George Reid, age 21, bass; Juan Pablo Izquierdo, conductor)
Concerto for Violin and Orchestra
    in B-Minor, Mvt. I. . . . . . . Saint-Saëns
(Young Uck Kim, age 19, violin; Leonard Bernstein, conductor)

38. Charles Ives: American Pioneer   February 23, 1967

ALL MUSIC BY IVES:

The Gong on the Hook and Ladder, or, The Fireman's Parade on Main
    Street
Washington's Birthday (from *Holiday Symphony*)
Song: "Lincoln, the Great Commoner"
(Simon Estes, bass-baritone, Leonard Bernstein at the piano)
The Circus Band
The Unanswered Question

39. Alumni Reunion   April 19, 1967

Variations on a Rococo Theme
(Var. I, III, V, VI, VII)   .   .   .   .   .   Tchaikovsky
(Stephen Kates, cello)
Mi chiamano Mimì, aria from
    La Bohème   .   .   .   .   Puccini
"My Man's Gone Now," aria from
    Porgy and Bess   .   .   .   .   .   .   Gershwin
(Veronica Tyler, soprano)
Piano Concerto No. 2 in B-flat Major   .   .   .   .   Brahms
(André Watts, piano)

40. A Toast to Vienna in
       3/4 Time   December 25, 1967

Wiener Blut   .   .   .   .   J. Strauss
Contradanz No. 3, K. 605   .   .   .   .   .   .   Mozart
Symphony No. 41, "Jupiter," Minuet   .   .   .   .   Mozart
Symphony No. 7, Scherzo   .   .   .   .   .   . Beethoven
Des Knaben Wunderhorn   .   .   .   .   .   .   Mahler
"*Rheinlegendchen*": Christa Ludwig soprano
"*Des Antonius von Padua Fischpredigt*": Walter Berry, baritone
"*Verlor'ne Müh' *": Miss Ludwig and Mr. Berry
Suite from *Der Rosenkavalier*   .   .   .   .   . R. Strauss

41. Forever Beethoven   January 28, 1968

ALL MUSIC BY BEETHOVEN:

Symphony No. 5 in C-Minor, Mvt. I
*Concerto No. 4 in G Major for Piano
    and Orchestra,* Mvts. II & III

356

(Joseph Kalichstein, piano; Paul Capolongo, conductor)
Leonore Overture No. 3

42. Young Performers No. 9   March 31, 1968

*Concerto in A-Minor for Cello
    and Orchestra* . . . . . . .Saint-Saëns
(Lawrence Foster, age 14, cello; Alois Springer, conductor)
Piano Pieces for Four Hands. . . . . . von Weber
Allegro/Turandot March/March in G Minor
(Martin and Steven Vann, age 17, piano)
*Symphonic Metamorphosis on Themes of
    Carl Maria von Weber* . . . . . . Hindemith
(Allegro conducted by Leonard Bernstein; Turandot March conducted
    by Helen Quach; March conducted by Mr. Bernstein)

43. Quiz-Concert: How Musical
    Are You?   May 26, 1968

Symphony No. 1, Chorale to end. . . . . Brahms
Overture: The Marriage of Figaro . . . . . Mozart
Classical Symphony, Mvt. I . . . . . . Prokofieff
Capriccio Espagnol, Gypsy Scene and
    Fandango . . . . Rimsky-Korsakoff

44. Fantastic Variations
    (*Don Quixote*)   December 25, 1968

ALL MUSIC FROM *DON QUIXOTE* BY
RICHARD STRAUSS:

Complete: Don Quixote Theme/Sancho Panza
    Theme
Variations I through II; Variation III (excerpt)
Variations IV through VII; Finale

45. Bach Transmogrified   April 27, 1969

Little Fugue in G-Minor . . . . Bach
Organ solo: Michael Korn
Orchestral transcription by
    Leopold Stokowski, conductor
Moog synthesizer transcription by Walter Sear

357

Partita in E-Major . . . . Bach
    Violin solo: David Nadien
Phorion [based on the *Partita*] (excerpts) . . . . Foss
Brandenburg Concerto No. 5, Mvt. I . . . . . Bach
Rock Variation and Fantasy by
    The New York Rock 'n' Roll Ensemble

46. Berlioz Takes a Trip   May 25, 1969

    Symphonie Fantastique . . . . . . Berlioz
    "Visions and Passions," Mvt. I (excerpts)
    "A Ball," Mvt. II
    "Scene in the Countryside," Mvt. III (excerpt)
    "March to the Scaffold," Mvt. IV
    "Nightmare of the Witches' Sabbath," Mvt. V

47. Two Ballet Birds   September 14, 1969

    Swan Lake . . . . Tchaikovsky
    Opening Act II
    Black Swan Pas de Deux (Act III)
    Introduction and Adagio
    Male Variation
    Female Variation
    Coda
    Firebird Suite . . . . Stravinsky
    Introduction and Firebird Variation
    Ronde of the Princesses
    Infernal Dance of King Kastchei
    Berceuse and Finale

48. *Fidelio:* A Celebration of Life   March 29, 1970

    Fidelio, Act II (excerpts) . . . . . Beethoven
    Aria: *Gott, welch Dunkel hier!*
        In des Lebens Frühlingstagen . . . . Florestan
    Duet: *Wie kalt ist es . . .*
        Nur hurtig fort . . . . Leonore, Rocco
    Trio: *Euch werde Lohn. . .* . . Florestan, Leonore, Rocco
    Quartet: *Er sterbe*
        Es schlägt der Rache Stunde . . Pizarro, Florestan,
                                 Leonore, Rocco
    Members of the American Opera Center at Juilliard:

Tito Capobianco, general Director
Florestan: Forest Warren
Leonore: Anita Darian
Rocco: Howard Ross
Pizarro: David Cumberland

49. The Anatomy of a
    Symphony Orchestra   May 24, 1970

   The Pines of Rome . . . . Respighi
       The Pines of the Villa Borghese
       Pines Near a Catacomb
       The Pines of the Janiculus
       The Pines of the Appian Way

50. A Copland Celebration   December 27, 1970

   MUSIC BY AARON COPLAND:

   Concerto for Clarinet and Orchestra
   (Stanley Drucker, soloist)
   Suite from the Ballet *Billy the Kid* (excerpts)
   Open Prairie
   Street in a Frontier Town
   Billy's Capture and Celebration
   Billy's Death (Pas de deux)
   Finale

51. Thus Spoke Richard Strauss   April 4, 1971

   Thus Spake Zarathustra . . . . . . Strauss

52. Liszt and the Devil   February 13, 1972

   Faust Symphony . . . . Liszt

359

53. Holst: *The Planets*   March 26, 1972

    I—Mars, the Bringer of War
    II—Venus, the Bringer of Peace
    III—Mercury, the Winged Messenger
    IV—Jupiter, the Bringer of Jollity
    V—Uranus, the Magician
    V—Pluto, the Unpredictable: Improvisation (not by Holst)

360

$\mathscr{L}$eonard Bernstein (1918–90)

Leonard Bernstein, born in Lawrence, Massachusetts, on August 25, 1918, began to develop his musical gifts at the age of ten, when by chance his family acquired a piano. His subsequent musical ambitions were discouraged by his father, Samuel J. Bernstein, a Russian-Jewish immigrant who in the Old Country had held musicians in low esteem. Samuel Bernstein did, however, instill a love for Jewish tradition, profoundly affecting a number of his son's compositions. Moreover, the sermons of Rabbi H. H. Rubenowitz (Temple Mishkan Tefila, Boston) enthralled the youngster, eventually influencing his clear expository style as an author. The compositions of the Temple's music director, Solomon Braslavsky, also made an impact on the budding musician.

Bernstein was the first internationally known musician to be wholly the product of American schooling. His primary education was at Garrison Grammar School, Roxbury, Massachusetts. He graduated from Boston Latin School in 1935, Harvard University in 1939 (A. Tillman

Merritt, harmony; Walter Piston, counterpoint and fugue; Edward B. Hill, orchestration), and the Curtis Institute of Music in Philadelphia in 1941 (Fritz Reiner, conducting; Randall Thompson, orchestration; Isabella Vengerova, piano). Keyboard studies had begun earlier in Boston with Helen Coates (later his secretary) and Heinrich Gebhard.

He made his unofficial conducting debut at Harvard in performances of his own incidental score to Aristophanes' *The Birds*, and of Blitzstein's musical play *The Cradle Will Rock* (both 1939). In the summers of 1940 and 1941 he studied at the Berkshire Music Center at Tanglewood, where, in 1942, he became assistant to Serge Koussevitzky, some of whose passionate conducting style and sense of mission he assimilated. He credited Philip Marson, his English teacher at Boston Latin School, with introducing him to the wonder of language, and David W. Prall at Harvard with broadening his aesthetic and philosophical horizons. Significantly, his compositions display a penchant for using texts or some form of program. As he wrote in the Foreword to his *The Age of Anxiety* (*Symphony No. 2*): "I have a deep suspicion that every work I write, for whatever medium, is really theater music in some way."

Bernstein became Assistant Conductor of the New York Philharmonic in 1943, and on the fourteenth of November made a spectacular debut, substituting on short notice for the ailing guest conductor, Bruno Walter. Thereafter, Bernstein was in great demand and toured worldwide with many other orchestras, conducting and sometimes doubling as piano soloist. Over the course of his entire conducting career, he led over seventy different professional orchestras, the most prominent among them being the New York Philharmonic, the Boston Symphony, the Israel Philharmonic, and the Vienna Philharmonic.

From 1945 to 1948 he headed the New York City Symphony, presenting many rarities. He taught part-time at Brandeis University (1951–55) and during the summers at Tanglewood, where he succeeded Koussevitzky in the conducting department.

During his forties (1958–69) he was Music Director of the New York Philharmonic. After this eleven-year tenure, he was named Laureate Conductor, and in 1971 led his one thousandth concert with the orchestra. He made more than four hundred recordings with the Philharmonic. His programs included much contemporary music, about two hundred works, with emphasis on the works of Stravinsky, Copland, and their followers (among them disciples of the French teacher Nadia Boulanger). But he showed less sympathy toward the Viennese school of Schoenberg and his followers. While his programming encompassed all aspects of the standard symphonic literature, he had a strong predilection for the music of Haydn, Beethoven, Brahms, Schumann, and Mahler. In fact, beginning in 1960, the worldwide renewal of interest in Mahler's works blossomed under Bernstein's missionary zeal. The same can be said of his enthusiasm for some of the orchestral works of Charles Ives.

Bernstein's natural affinity for teaching found its greatest fulfillment on television, beginning with ten appearances on the "Omnibus" series (1954–61) and fifteen programs for adults with the New York Philharmonic (1958–62). Also in 1958 he undertook the series of televised "Young People's Concerts," which lasted until 1972 (fifty-three different programs), making a major impact on American culture. He often appeared on "Great Performances," in programs such as *Bernstein's Beethoven* and *Brahms/Bernstein*. Concerts of Bernstein's and other composers' works (Stravinsky, Copland, Elgar, Shostakovich, Haydn, Mahler, Ives, et al.) were also captured on video for future generations.

His "Omnibus" scripts became a bestseller when published as part of *The Joy of Music* (1959). This was followed by four other books: the first edition of *Leonard Bernstein's Young People's Concerts for Reading and Listening* (1962), *The Infinite Variety of Music* (1966), and *Findings* (1982). Probably his most significant contribution to musical thought is his book *The Unanswered Question* (1976), based on the six Charles Eliot Norton Lectures he delivered at Harvard in 1973. All of these have been translated into numerous foreign languages.

Elsewhere, student instrumentalists and conductors were the beneficiaries of his extraordinary teaching skills over the years: in the United States at the Tanglewood Music Center and at the Los Angeles Philharmonic Institute, which he helped found in 1982; in Germany at the Schleswig-Holstein Music Festival, which he helped create in 1986; in Italy at the Accademia di Santa Cecilia in Rome; and in Japan at the Pacific Music Festival, also begun with his leadership in 1990.

Leonard Bernstein was one of very few composers who was equally at home in the popular theater and the concert hall. He made substantial contributions to the Broadway musical stage: *On the Town* (1944); *Wonderful Town* (1953); *Candide* (1956), which, through various transformations, has become a staple for opera companies; and the now classic *West Side Story* (1957; the film version won ten Academy Awards in 1961). In addition, there is his *Mass: A Theater Piece for Singers, Players and Dancers*, composed at the request of Mrs. John F. Kennedy for the opening of the Kennedy Center in 1971; the one-act opera *Trouble in Tahiti* (1952), subsequently incorporated into the three-act opera *A Quiet Place* (1983); and the Bicentennial work *1600 Pennsylvania Avenue* (1976). He collaborated with choreographer Jerome Robbins in three major ballets: *Fancy Free* (1944), *Facsimile* (1946), and *Dybbuk* (1974). Robbins also choreographed the composer's *The Age of Anxiety*. Other choreographers (John Neumeier, Margo Sappington, Todd Bolender, Edward Villella among them) have created dance pieces to almost all of the Bernstein concert works. One of these, *Prelude, Fugue and Riffs*, has had (as of 1991) ten different choreographic treatments. He wrote the score for the Academy Award–winning film *On the Waterfront* (1954), from which a concert suite was derived, and the incidental scores for several Broadway productions, including *Peter Pan* (1950) and *The Lark* (1955, transformed into *Missa Brevis*, 1988).

Much of the show music demonstrated his allegiance to New York City and its environs: *On the Town*, *Fancy Free*, *Wonderful Town*, *West Side Story*, *On the Waterfront*, and, arguably, *Trouble in Tahiti*, and *A Quiet Place*. Virtually all his works have been recorded by him.

Stylistically, he was more a consolidator than an innovator in his works for the concert hall; and, as such, he was an unabashed eclectic. His prominent influences were Stravinsky, Copland, Blitzstein, Hindemith, and Shostakovich; and the lesser ones included Richard Strauss, Mahler, and Berg. Added to this were jazz idioms, Latin-Americn rhythms, and the occasional use of twelve-tone and aleatoric procedures (but always in the context of tonality, which he felt was "built in to the human organism"). In *Songfest* (1977), for example, the eclecticism is manifested in the highly diversified characterizations with which he musically portrays the poetry of thirteen Americans. Even in the early *Clarinet Sonata* (1942), passages redolent of the Hindemith sound comfortably share quarters with jazzy neighbors. And one of his last works, *Arias and Barcarolles* (1988), contains American-sounding "Coplandisms" alongside Viennese atonalisms. In his operetta *Candide* he was able to indulge his eclectic proclivities to the hilt, since the globe-trotting plot allowed him to make a pastiche of many different national styles.

Although there is an element of Shostakovich in *Jeremiah* (*Symphony No. 1*, winner of the New York Music Critics' Circle Award, 1943), the Bernstein voice is considerably stronger, as evoked through childhood memories of Jewish song. Other aspects of his Jewish-cultural conditions are to be found in *Kaddish* (*Symphony No. 3*), *Chichester Psalms*, the ballet *Dybbuk*, the flute concerto *Halil*, and the orchestral work *Concerto for Orchestra* (*"Jubilee Games"*), as well as in various songs and choral pieces. Most fascinating is the hidden Jewish symbolism to be found in the piano concerto/symphony *The Age of Anxiety*.

Rhythm in Bernstein's music is particularly striking, showing a predilection for syncopation, cross-rhythms, and asymmetric meters in slow and fast tempos, as, for example, in *Serenade for Violin, Strings and Percussion* (1954), *Divertimento for Orchestra* (1980), and other works. His melodies place architectonic importance on short motives, with some of the theater works exploiting only one basic interval. His orchestration displays a conspicuous use of solo piano, brass in high registers, and a large virtuosic percussion section.

The stage works contain an unusual degree of formal cohesion. *Trouble in Tahiti* is symmetrically organized into seven scenes; *Fancy Free* is a set of seven vignettes in rondo design; *Facsimile* is actually an A-B-A symphonic movement in which all the melodic material grows out of the opening phrases. Bernstein also cultivated a concatenation technique of melodic variation, with musical ideas evolving from each other (as in the metamorphosis "warm-worm-word-cord-cold" or in "more-lore-lose-loss-less"). *The Age of Anxiety* was the first work to use this procedure. In the score to *On the Waterfront*, a barbaric fugue is gradually transformed into a lyric love theme through such chain-reaction devices. In *Kaddish*, similarly, an angular twelve-tone row is metamorphosed into a tonal canon for boys' choir.

The composer was a man of immense energy who worked best against a deadline. The musical *Wonderful Town* was written in five weeks; the *Slava!, A Political Overture* in only one. Four of the more disparate works overlapped each other in various stages of development: *Candide*, *Serenade for Violin, Strings and Percussion*, *On the Waterfront*, and *West Side Story*.

Critics, especially in the 1950s, questioned Bernstein's wide-ranging activities, claiming he would have become a better musician if he had concentrated on only one musical discipline to the exclusion of the others. If he had followed their advice, however, he would have ceased to be himself. Early on, he stated: "I want to keep on trying to be, in the full sense of that wonderful word, a musician. I also want to teach. I want to write books and poetry. And I think I can still do justice to them all."

In his lifetime, Bernstein was the recipient of twenty-three honorary degrees; thirteen foreign government decorations; thirteen Grammy Awards, including a Lifetime Achievement Grammy in 1985; sixteen platinum/gold and international record awards; eleven Emmy Awards;

367

ten miscellaneous television awards; over fifty arts awards, including the Gold Medal from the American Academy of Arts and Letters, the MacDowell Colony Gold Medal, the Handel Medallion, a Tony Award, the Theater Hall of Fame, Kennedy Center Honors; twenty-two civic awards; at least fifteen honorary memberships in various societies; and four honorary presidencies or laureate conductorships. The last award Bernstein received during his lifetime was in 1990—the Praemium Imperiale, a Japanese international prize awarded for lifetime achievement in the arts. He used the prize to found the Bernstein Education Through the Arts (BETA) Fund. Posthumous awards continue to be named in his honor and memory.

Humanitarian concerns, especially for human rights and world peace, were passionately articulated by him in various forums, including houses of worship and academic convocations. His 1985 "Journey for Peace" tour to Hiroshima with the European Community Orchestra marked the fortieth anniversary of the first atomic bombing; and in 1989 his worldwide "September 1, 1939" telecast from Warsaw remembered the invasion of Poland by the Nazis fifty years earlier. On Christmas Day 1989, Bernstein led a historic concert celebrating the dismantling of the Berlin Wall.

A strong supporter of Amnesty International, Leonard Bernstein established, for its benefit in 1987, the Felicia Montealegre Fund, in memory of his wife, the Chilean-born actress whom he married in 1951. Mrs. Bernstein died in 1978. He died twelve years later, on October 14, 1990. They were the parents of three children: Jamie, Alexander, and Nina; and the grandparents of two: Francisca and Evan.

—J.G., 1992

About the Editor

Composer, author, and lecturer Jack Gottlieb was Leonard Bernstein's assistant, then editor, from 1958 to Bernstein's death in 1990—with a few years off for good behavior. Currently he is an archivist for the Bernstein Estate. He has edited the complete catalog of Bernstein's works, written numerous concert and recording notes about his music, and edited the first three of his books. Gottlieb is also the author of scholarly articles on general musical topics, a lecturer on the Jewish influence on American popular music, and the composer of theater works (words and music), numerous choral pieces and songs, chamber music, and Jewish liturgical music. The 1991 CD recording *Evening, Morn & Noon— The Sacred Music of Jack Gottlieb* is dedicated to Bernstein's memory. Jack Gottlieb is president of the American Society for Jewish Music.

*A*cknowledgments

Many thanks to the following for permission to reprint excerpts from copyright material included in this book:

"All Shook Up." Words and Music by Otis Blackwell and Elvis Presley. Copyright © 1957 by Shalimar Music Corporation. Copyright Renewed and Assigned to Elvis Presley Music (Administered by R&H Music.) International Copyright Secured. All Rights Reserved.

"Along Comes Mary." Words and Music by Tandyn Almer. Copyright © 1965 by Irving Music, Inc. (BMI). All Rights Reserved. International Copyright Secured.

American Festival Overture by William Schuman. Copyright 1941 by G. Schirmer, Inc. Reprinted by permission.

"And I Love Her." Words and Music by John Lennon and Paul McCartney. Copyright © 1964 by NORTHERN SONGS. All Rights Controlled and Administered by MCA MUSIC PUBLISHING, A Division of MCA, INC., 1755 Broadway, New York, NY 10019 under license from NORTHERN SONGS. International Copyright Secured. All Rights Reserved.

Billy the Kid by Aaron Copland. Copyright Renewed. Reprinted by permission of the Copyright owner and Boosey & Hawkes, Inc., Sole Licensee.

"Bugle Call Rag" by Jack Pettis, Billy Meyers, Elmer Schoebel. Copyright 1923 (Renewed 1951) by Mills Music, Inc., New York, NY. Used by Permission. All Rights Reserved. International Copyright Secured. Made in USA.

370

372

Index